THE GLOBAL HISTORY SERIES

Leften Stavrianos, *Northwestern University*
General Editor

This series aims to present history in global perspective, going beyond national or regional limitations, and dealing with overriding trends and forces. The various collections of original materials span the globe, range from prehistoric times to the present, and include anthropology, economics, political science, and religion, as well as history.

Franklin D. Scott, the editor of this volume, is Professor of History at Northwestern University. He is the author of *The United States and Scandinavia, American Experience of Swedish Students, Emigration and Immigration,* and *Wertmuller: Artist and Immigrant Farmer.* He has written numerous articles for professional journals.

Also in the Global History Series

Africa in the Days of Exploration, *edited by Roland Oliver and Caroline Oliver,* S-123

The Americas on the Eve of Discovery, *edited by Harold E. Driver,* S-93

Asia on the Eve of Europe's Expansion, *edited by Donald F. Lach and Carol Flaumenhaft,* S-125

Christianity in the Non-Western World, *edited by Charles W. Forman,* S-150

The Decline of Empires, *edited by S. N. Eisenstadt,* S-154

European Expansion and the Counter-Example of Asia, *edited by Joseph R. Levenson,* S-170

Man Before History, *edited by Creighton Gabel,* S-92

The Muslim World on the Eve of Europe's Expansion, *edited by John J. Saunders,* S-144

The Political Awakening of Africa, *edited by Rupert Emerson and Martin Kilson,* S-124

Russia's Eastward Expansion, *edited by George Alexander Lensen,* S-94

WORLD MIGRATION
IN MODERN TIMES

WORLD MIGRATION
IN MODERN TIMES

EDITED BY FRANKLIN D. SCOTT

Prentice-Hall, Inc. / *Englewood Cliffs, N.J.*

137106

Library of Congress Catalog Card Number 68-27492.

Printed in the United States of America.

Current printing (last number):
10 9 8 7 6 5 4 3 2 1

To the uprooted and the transplanted

PREFACE

The purpose of this collection of essays is to provide a sampling of the vast literature on migration and, hopefully, thus to stimulate further reading and research. I am grateful to many students and assistants who in various ways have helped to identify effective selections from out of a vast storehouse. Especially to be thanked are Carl Brodin, Linda Duke, Rilla Ekholm, Peter Findlay, Christine McHugh, Jerry D. McCoy, and Judith Carroll Stull.

F. D. S.

CONTENTS

INTRODUCTION   1

1 / Migration in the Dynamics of History, *Franklin D. Scott*   1

I / EUROPEAN EMIGRATION AND AMERICAN
IMMIGRATION   9

2 / The Great Migration from Europe, *Franklin D. Scott*   9
3 / The Peopling of the American Colonies, *Marcus Lee Hansen*   12
4 / What is an American?, *J. Hector St. John Crèvecoeur*   16
5 / The German Background of Emigration, *Mack Walker*   19
6 / Irish Emigration, *Arnold Schrier*   24
7 / The Mennonites of Alexanderwohl, *Frederick A. Norwood*   31
8 / The Atlantic Crossing, *Edwin C. Guillet*   33
9 / Problems of Adjustment, *Oscar Handlin*   38
10 / The Tree that Barely Leafs, *Arthur Landfors*   43
11 / The United States and Italy: Migration and Repatriation,
George R. Gilkey   44
12 / The M-Factor in American History, *George W. Pierson*   51

II / LATIN AMERICAN MIGRATION   59

13 / Peopling the Pampa, *Mark Jefferson*   60

14 / Immigrants and Their Assimilation in Brazil,
Emilio Willems   65
15 / New Patterns, *Anthony T. Bouscaren*   73

III / AFRICAN MIGRATION   81

16 / Expansion of the Bantu, *Roland Oliver*   81
17 / African Negroes to the Americas, *Stanley Elkins*   87
18 / The *Oibu-Dudu* (White-Black) Immigrants to Lagos,
Nigeria, *Spencer H. Brown*   94
19 / Migrations to the Pare Mountains, *Isaria Kimambo*   96
20 / Emigration and Return of the Chagga, *Susan Geiger Rogers*   102
21 / The Great Trek, *Eric Walker*   111

IV / ASIAN MIGRATION   119

22 / Asia on the Move, *Bruno Lasker*   119
23 / "The Birth of Two Nations"—The Indian-Pakistani
Exchange after World War II, *Margaret Bourke-White*   127
24 / Australia and the Restriction of Asian Immigration,
A. T. Yarwood   131
25 / Chinese Migration to the United States, *Gunther Barth*   137

V / CONTEMPORARY MIGRATION   145

26 / Mass Migration Then and Now, *C. P. Kindleberger*   145
27 / Refugee Migration in the Twentieth Century,
Louise Holborn   153
28 / Israeli Melting Pot, *Hal Lehrman*   159

VI / CONCLUSION   167

29 / The Global Redistribution of Man, *L. S. Stavrianos*   167

FURTHER READING 175

Maps

Bantu Expansion 85
Racial Distribution in the World, 15th Century 172
Racial Distribution in the World, 20th Century 173

INTRODUCTION

1 / MIGRATION IN THE DYNAMICS OF HISTORY

Ever since Adam and Eve were forced out of the Garden of Eden, men have been on the move, and movement has spread culture and stimulated invention. When man is mobile he meets other men, and sparks fly between brains as well as between swords. Constant confrontation with new situations in nature and in social relationships demands adaptation and creativity, leads to invention and development. And when a group of people reaches the end of the road, settles down for long periods and loses contact with men moving about, that group stagnates. Most backward people on earth are the Indians of Tierra del Fuego, the Bushmen in the interior of South Africa, and the isolated tribes of aborigines in Australia. Within the United States the twelve poorest counties are neither Negro nor immigrant; they are almost pure old-line American stock that has stood still. Civilization is a product of mobility and the crossroads, of the ever shifting population of cities.

Although we lack precise records of the early migrations of men, the evidence of legends and archaeology indicates not only that peoples have moved from time immemorial, but that they have maintained the memory of movement. The Goths of the Ukraine retained a belief that their ancestors came from the north in great white birds. For the Etruscans we have chiefly the record of archaeology, but it is a rich one. For the migrations of the post-Columbian world we have a full account of travel and migration, the record of a vast centrifugal move-

Franklin D. Scott, *Migration in the Dynamics of History.* Copyright © 1965 by the Department of History, Municipal University of Omaha. A published lecture, condensed.

ment out of Europe with which we yet live—so much so that we tend to take it for granted.

Migration has been such a universal phenomenon that some scholars have speculated that it is instinctive in man, as it is in many animals, birds, and fish—the reindeer that lead the Lapps from the lichen of northern Sweden to the summer grass of northern Norway and back again, the salmon that go off into the deep ocean and two years later smell their way back to their spawning grounds, the birds that fly long seasonal migrations and reappear on schedule. Is it possible that for man himself the search for variety as well as the need to change hunting grounds or pasture lands has bred some innate urge for movement?

But there are certain main types of human migration with which we are concerned.

First we may note examples of creeping expansion. The Slavs thus at one time pressed westward in Europe as far as the Elbe, and then the Germans, growing in numbers and strength, applied a counter pressure that slowly gave them the lands eastward through Prussia and northward into the Baltic provinces. Thus, too, the Chinese moved slowly southward into Southeast Asia and northward into Manchuria. In South Africa the Zulus moved in from the north, and then the Boers pushed northward into the *veld*. Possibly this creeping expansion is best illustrated by certain tribes of southern Kenya as described by Monica Hunter Wilson. It was customary among them, as villages grew in size and as young people grew to maturity, for the new generations to move out and organize new communities, sometimes just beyond the parent villages, more often leapfrogging over one or two neighboring villages and establishing new settlements on the "frontier." This may well have been the way the Goths moved south across Europe into the Ukraine, and the way African tribes moved westward across the Sudan. It reminds us also of the westward movement within the United States that, speeded by the railway, brought settlers tumbling out of Vermont to Pennsylvania, then a new generation on to Indiana or Illinois, and the next to Nebraska or Wyoming. In Nebraska, for example, the name of the town Ohiowa preserves the memory of its early settlers coming direct from Iowa or leapfrogging all the way from Ohio. The suburbs of our modern cities illustrate a somewhat similar pattern of expansion.

A second type of migration is the sharp, thin thrust: So we may characterize the sea movements of the Greeks to Syracuse, to Alexandria, to Marseilles, and to the coast of Spain, making a kind of

Greek fringe all around the Mediterranean. This was the nature of the Polynesian migration to Hawaii. And it is the name for the spectacular thrusts of the Vikings as they swept in their longboats to establish beachheads in Ireland and Normandy and Iceland, far around to Sicily, and in feebler thrusts to Greenland and the shores of North America. They struck also deep into Russia, where they organized the state and were gradually absorbed by the bulk of the Slavs. Movements such as these, though limited in time and numbers, nevertheless left lasting impact.

Third, and most impressive among the major types of migration is the bold mass movement of peoples, the *Völkerwanderung*. Such was the prehistoric Mediterranean transfer of the Etruscans from their home in Asia Minor, stopping possibly in Egypt, then moving on to central Italy, providing the base of technical and organizational skill on which the Latins were to build the Roman Republic. Then, after the Republic had become the Roman Empire, and when it weakened internally, the impact of the Teutonic migrations helped to give it the *coup de grâce* and to inject new blood. The cultural bridges established between the Roman and the Germanic worlds helped then to spread Christianity and the Latin language to northern Europe and to lay the foundations for pan-European Christendom. The complex dynamics of history can here be seen as a kind of chain reaction in which migration was one of the essential impulses.

Even vaster in both numbers of people and distance traveled was the mass movement from Europe overseas, a migration spanning four centuries and all the continents, but concentrated especially in the hundred years from 1830 to 1930, and two-thirds of it being migration from Europe to the United States. In that single century some 60,000,-000 men, women, and children left Europe, and 40,000,000 of them cast off forever the ties of home, family, and fatherland. They populated the prairies, raised wheat for the factory workers of their European homelands, developed new forms of government, and invented new machines and new gadgets, not only for themselves but to sell to the peoples across the oceans. This eventuated in speeding up the processes of change, in creating a "new world" in both Europe and America, and finally in extending this new civilization into the older continents of Africa and of Asia—revolutionizing the planet.

Enfolded more or less within these three broad categories are almost infinite varieties of migratory phenomena: forced migration such as the expulsion of the Huguenots and the African slave trade, conquest migration such as that of the hordes of Genghis Khan, conquest in the name of religion like the expansion of Islam, group religious migration like that of the Mennonites, Crusades like the push of the Teutonic knights into Prussia and the Baltic lands, or agreed transfers of population.

Of all the movements we have conjured up, some of them devastating in their original impact, is there even one that can be clearly branded, in the final balance, as destructive? It is the movement of people that has transformed the prairies from the hunting grounds of barbarians to farms and cities, factories and universities. If in some cases older cultures were obliterated in the process, then we must lay in the scales the cultures of the Aztecs and of the Sioux, for instance, and weigh them against their replacements.

It may appear that I am trying to build up migration as the great single cause of historic events. Not at all. Many factors—economic, geographic, technical, spiritual—are involved in human progress. The point is chiefly that migration is an activating factor. In the dynamics of historical development progress stems from one of two roots: Diffusion (or borrowing) is one; invention (or creativity) is the other. MIGRATION BOTH FACILITATES BORROWING AND STIMULATES CREATIVITY.

Borrowing, or diffusion of culture, is an obvious contribution of migration. As far back as the Stone Age wanderers took burial customs and styles for stone axes over long distances in northern Europe. Religion has been spread by individuals and by armies of migrants— Judaism to all corners of the world, Islam with irresistible force and persuasion across north Africa and far into Asia. Christianity has expanded with trade and military activity, and by missionaries inspired by the command "Go ye into all the earth and preach the gospel." Agricultural products and techniques were diffused by ancient peoples— wheat from Asia to northern Europe, manioc and rice from the East to Africa, cotton from South Africa to Egypt and Arabia (much later to America), cocoa by missionaries from South America to Africa, the potato from South America to Europe, horses from Europe to America —and by this grand-scale interchange everywhere more people have been able to live better. As to architecture, we need cite only the transition of the classic style from Greece westward through Europe and on to America and the rapid spread across the plains of the log cabin brought by immigrants from Finland and Sweden. In music, from spirituals to jazz, America is indebted to the unwilling immigrants from Africa, and the world is indebted for the newer developments born in the mixed society.

Bantu languages have been diffused by migrants through Africa, and European languages have affected all parts of the world—Portugese in large parts of Africa, in Brazil, and in various ports of Asia; Spanish through much of South and Central America and the Philippines; English in North America, South Africa, India. In its migration language, like the other things mentioned, has undergone change, has taken on new shades of meaning to express new attitudes and needs. English in America, for example, has come to reflect the restlessness and movement characteristic of the American scene. Struck with this, George Pierson has gone to his dictionaries and found an almost endless play of variations in the use of the word *go*.

Americans can go—all out, all the way, to pieces, or around in circles; bughouse, haywire, or nuts; bad, blooey, boom, or broke; hog-wild, head over heels, great guns, lickety-split, or like a bat out of hell. They can go steady, straight, sour, or wrong. They can go their own sweet way and tell others to go fly a kite, jump in the lake, peddle their papers, or (more insultingly) go way back and sit down. We will go down the line for a friend; go for six or a sleighride; go it alone, or one better; go off the rail or one's rocker; go on the loose, a bender, the rocks, or the wagon; go out of circulation, go the distance, works, or whole hog; go to bat for, to beat the band, to the races, to the mat, or to the wall; go up the spout or the river.

And Pierson reminds us of that subtle difference between England and the United States remarked by Mencken—that an Englishman stands for Parliament, whereas an American runs for Congress.

When a man travels, or when he moves, he takes with him what he can, but his baggage cannot hold everything. He meets new situations and is forced to make new tools and new institutions to cope with change. Creativity or invention is most vigorous where the challenge of the new situation is strongest (if not too strong). As Toynbee has pointed out, Iceland developed in the Middle Ages a political and literary culture superior to that of old Scandinavia because of the challenge of the new environment. Creativity that builds on past experience but that goes far beyond borrowing is evident in many aspects of immigrant societies. The United States affords illustrations.

Innovations in government began with the immigrants on the Mayflower, who found themselves separated from established authority and drew up their own Compact to guide them. Ideas of government without kings, and of division of powers, had been adumbrated in Europe. In America such revolutionary concepts could be put into practice, and fresh institutions could be created. When chartered companies or governments across the Atlantic attempted to dictate how the colonists should plant their crops or to direct their trade, it quickly became clear that they were unaware of conditions. Since neither the traditional ruler nor an upper-class elite was present in the new land, and since decisions had to be made, self-reliance was forced upon the settlers. The frontier equality of both need and opportunity bred democracy and eventually town-meeting and representative government. Experimentation led to the development of new crops and soon to crossbreeding and the creation of new species. Demand for new tools and weapons, and large quantities of them, produced not only the cotton gin, but the idea of interchangeable parts and mass production. Soon we had guns and wagons and automobiles and airplanes made on the production line. And it was no accident that it was in the United States, a country of immigration where the talents of diverse nationalities were mobilized, that atomic fission was achieved through the co-operative efforts of scientists from twelve countries.

The combined and often overlapping forces of diffusion and creativity build new cultures. Confrontation in migration of different people's and customs and ideas is perpetually provocative; so that of an immigrant society such as that in early America Tocqueville could note that the American "grows accustomed to change." Once having moved, it is easier to move again; restlessness breeds more restlessness and a readiness to change cars, styles, refrigerators, houses. In American cities oftentimes the average length of residence in one dwelling is three years. Like the Arabs we move our tents with the greatest ease. In America, to which men have traveled thousands of miles to "settle down," they and their descendants are constantly on the move. Forty per cent of all Americans over age fifty live in states other than their state of birth; few indeed live all their lives in the "old home town."

> Something hidden. Go and find it.
> Go and look behind the Ranges—
> Something lost behind the Ranges
> Lost and waiting for you. Go!

This is what George Pierson calls the "mobility factor" (or simply the "M-factor") in American history, one of the dynamic forces shaping the American character. It led to easy acquaintanceship, but to a difficult deepening of acquaintanceship into friendship. It meant a shifting of values, with a new emphasis on adjustment and change and with a de-emphasis on the things associated with an established community— things like the prestige of family, for example. If Descartes could say

"I think, therefore I am," the American may say, "I move, therefore I am alive."

The mobility of diverse peoples means also the blending of blood —and of languages and religions and customs. It happens in all lands. America is the example par excellence of the mixing process, and here some glory in it, some deplore it. Some, like the Mennonites, can by group solidarity and exclusiveness prevent the working of natural forces at least for a time, but the threat (for them) is powerful. At a recent meeting of the American Historical Association, Jewish and Irish scholars discussed the process, the Irish priding themselves on their achievements in being assimilated in intermarriage, in rising to high positions in government, and in becoming fused into American life. The Jewish scholar bemoaned the success of the Jews in finance and in the Hollywood arts, for success in assimilation means less of Jewishness. The process continues inevitably whatever the attitude of observers.

In one of the numerous re-examinations of the Turner hypothesis Everett Lee has suggested that Turner picked the wrong factor to explain his phenomena. Although migration is not the sole explanation of American development, it probably is a better one than is the frontier. The geographic frontier was a passing phenomenon. The true safety valve for the American East and for discontented Europe was migration—migration to better farms, migration to cities and factories, migration overseas, anywhere. For now, long after the geographic frontier is gone, migration continues to shift people about, to relieve some societies of a burden and to provide others with the hands and heads needed for productivity. As long as men can move they are free, they have choices and therefore can have hope. We can now see, more readily than Turner could, the importance of movement rather than merely land, because within our day the pattern of migration has been revolutionized.

Nineteenth-century migration took people from developed countries to the empty spaces of new continents; it took them in large masses across wide oceans; it attracted chiefly the vigorous but untrained laboring classes; it was at first agricultural, then industrial. But now the day of intercontinental mass migration has passed. Nation states carefully select the immigrants they will admit. In Europe the movement is from countries little developed industrially to those already highly developed, like Germany, Switzerland, Sweden. In Britain and several of the continental countries it is a two-way flow, bringing in needed unskilled labor, as from Jamaica to England, and exporting to the United States highly trained engineers and scientists. In Africa the wealth of labor is not moving away to places where there are factories and farms, but instead technicians are moving to Africa to build new plants and to utilize the labor on the spot. Skilled labor is now more mobile than the unskilled. Countries like Germany and the United States exchange different kinds of experts, and even small countries like Denmark and Belgium are now sending out not colonial administrators or unemployed workers, but engineers and industrial managers.

Hence migration adapts itself to economic fluctuations and the nationalistic demands of new countries. Whether it creeps or whether it thrusts, or if it overwhelms with mass, if it moves from metropolis to colony or back and forth, or meets changed circumstances with a reversal of flow, it still, as in the nineteenth century and earlier, unites the experience of established societies with the resources of the newer lands, carries energizing currents in both directions, dynamizes the processes of history.

2 / THE GREAT MIGRATION FROM EUROPE

The Great Migration was the accumulation of millions of individual and small group movements; it extended over a period of four centuries; it took some 68,000,000 people from Europe and scattered them literally over the earth; it gave birth to new nations and roused old nations from their torpor; it Europeanized the world so well that "the lesser breeds without the law" (to use the phrase of Kipling, poet of empire) have adopted Europe's methods to throw Europe back on her heels; and thus the remarkable epoch of European expansion, colonization, emigration, has come to an end.

This tremendous migratory surge began when Europe discovered the "great frontier" of America and the other sparsely peopled lands such as Australia and South Africa. It was associated with the decline of feudalism in Europe, and it has hastened the end of feudal society —for migration is a feature of a free society; bondage to the land cannot survive when man is free to move. The tempo of movement was accelerated with increasing freedom, with new developments in shipping and means of communication, and with a complex and cumulative host of factors repelling people from the Old World and attracting them to the New. But certain broad and fundamental causes underlay the entire phenomenon.

The most powerful factor impelling emigration was an extraordinary increase in population, *preceding* the ability of agriculture to feed it or of industry to give it jobs. In 1650 approximately 545,000,000 human beings lived on this planet; 300 years later the number had

Adapted from Franklin D. Scott, *Emigration and Immigration* (Washington, 1963), 2–5. Reprinted by permission of the American Historical Association.

grown to about 2,500,000,000—more than a four-fold increase. Europe's people increased from *c.* 100,000,000 to 560,000,000, and during the same period she was sending abroad *permanently* some 40,000,000. Without the safety valve of the "great frontier," would Europe have suffered the crowding and the famines and the cultural slowdown of Asia? We cannot know. We do know that as the death rate declined, and before the birth rate responded to keep things in balance, emigration skimmed off a significant portion of the surplus. This not only relieved Europe's numbers, but in transoceanic fields the emigrants from Europe raised wheat to feed the people who stayed home.

The population problem went hand in hand with economic pressures—occasionally in the stark form of hunger. The potato blight of the 1840's hit western Europe hard, and it left many an Irishman with the simple choice between starvation and emigration. Fortunately the pressures of hunger and joblessness were usually less severe. More often they acted as on a young Swede, one of seven sons, who saw that the patrimony would be too small for seven new families; against his father's will he crossed the sea, and he was one of the happy ones who made a fortune. The general operation of economic causation is illustrated by the fluctuations in the stream of emigration: it was shallowest during periods of prosperity in Europe and depression in the United States, and it swelled to a flood when Europe faced hard times and America rode a crest of prosperity. But variations and contradictions arose, too, from local conditions and from individual sectors of the economy.

This phenomenon of the business cycle in relation to migration indicates also that the causes of migration were located both in the country of origin and in the country of destination. Neither the push nor the pull functioned alone. Reasons there had to be for disappointment and frustration at home, but also reasons for hope in the new country. There appears to be a correlation not only with temporary swings of the economic pendulum, but with the stages of economic development. If one takes W. W. Rostow's chart of the "Stages," he can see that for four countries at least (Germany, Sweden, Russia, and Japan) the flood tide of emigration coincided with the take-off into industrialization—in other words, the largest emigration came at just that moment when the old economic order was giving way to the new, and when there was maximum disturbance of employment. (This hypothesis calls for careful research.) Basic economic factors were also indicated by the fact that it was neither the wealthy nor the very poor who left their homelands. The wealthy had too much at stake to tear up roots; the extremely poor had neither the passage money nor the stamina nor the vision to undertake the great adventure. The vast majority of emigrants were therefore from the lower-middle economic strata, people who had a little but had an appetite for more. Of the multitude of other causative forces, besides population and economics, the most important was probably religion. The Jews at repeated times, from the Diaspora to the return to Israel, illustrated the religious motivation. The motives of both Pilgrims and Puritans were fundamentally religious. Groups like these were exercising their rights to flee from oppression, to seek freedom. In other cases the demand was for political freedom, as with refugees from the 1848 revolutions, from Nazi Germany in the 1930's, from Communist Russia after 1917. Often migration was literally forced, as in the Greco-Turkish exchange of populations after World War I and the great refugee movements after World War II. These and other general factors, such as the desire to escape military service, appeared as causes for large numbers of emigrants, but purely personal causes were also effective.

The great migration of the nineteenth and twentieth centuries was a movement of individuals. Each person had to make his own decision even if he came with a group. And millions came entirely alone. They were affected by the deep-seated social causes of migration, but they were more immediately driven by the circumstances of their own lives, by factors such as disappointment in love, a brush with the police, a dispute with the boss, an overbearing father, or an urge for adventure. Reasons and combinations of reasons could be numbered to infinity. The only factors universally applicable were dissatisfaction with things as they were and hope in what might be elsewhere.

Most of these millions of emigrants were young—the bulk of them in the 15 to 35 year age bracket. And most were male (85 per cent in the case of the early Austrian emigration), especially in the late nineteenth-century rush as new nationalities suddenly awoke to the call of the New World. The proportion of the sexes evened out after the first or second decade when the men of the advance guard had saved enough money to send for sweethearts or families, or when demand for domestic servants provided jobs for girls. Some of them were rebels and misfits in their own countries; practically all were the unhappy, the propertyless or dispossessed, the restless and frustrated. But for the most part these same people were also the virile, the industrious, the hopeful, men with vision and drive and a love of adventure, men who could look to the future, strong young men.

As they became immigrants in a new land, some, even of the strong, were broken by the magnitude of the task or by sheer ill fortune. Others less hardy found themselves misfits and disappointed wherever they went; by migration they only exchanged one set of adversities for another. The new slums might be worse than the old, or the isolation of the frontier could be unbearable. Some suffered massacre by Indians, others died in malarial swamps, more were broken by the competitive struggle in factories and offices. Several millions returned more or less quietly to their homes, others kept moving on and on, searching and hoping until they died. The totality of disillusionments and calamities was at least a third of the immigrant flow. But these, like the casualties of an army, were sloughed off; these were not the men and women who left the lasting impact. Perhaps they should have a monument, but the successful survivors would have to build it.

It was the legion of survivors that peopled the empty spaces of the earth, that took European culture to Australia and South America, South Africa and North America, and in the new environments adapted and transformed their old institutions and ideas. They pioneered the pampas or the prairies, or they restored the farms abandoned by onward-moving earlier settlers. They conquered lands from Indians or Hottentots or Kaffirs. They built railroads and stoked factory furnaces and did domestic chores. They set up shops that grew into stores, they made watches and glass and clothes, they built bridges and buildings, they mined coal and gold and diamonds. They established churches and schools and newspapers. They brought with them dreams and skills and muscles. They made towns and cities. The newcomers faced tensions and misunderstandings, not only with natives, but also with older settlers—difficulties often exacerbated by differences in language and background and by the common struggle up from poverty. But gradually they learned to work together, to tolerate if not to understand the differences among them. They developed new interests and new loyalties. They intermarried and produced new blends both biologically and culturally.

Of all this infinite variety and complexity the following selections can give but a few glimpses.

3 / THE PEOPLING OF THE AMERICAN COLONIES

For the setting in which the European colonization of North America began, let us turn to the account of Marcus Lee Hansen, a scholar who

*but for his untimely death probably would have given us a definitive
narrative and analysis of American immigration.*

The twelve hundred miles of coast line stretching northward from
Spanish Florida was not the scene of the first British ventures in
colonization. Experience elsewhere had already established the practices to be followed. Lawyers of the Crown were skilled in drawing
up charters; merchants knew how to promote the sale of company
shares; and in every port of the south and west of England courageous
adventurers stood ready to embark on any enterprise offering a prospect of excitement and a little gold. As yet, however, no policy had
been devised to secure for remote plantations a population of British
subjects fitted to reduce the wilderness to cultivation.

The earlier companies organized to trade in the Levant and the
European north had evolved many features later adopted by colonizing
groups, but these companies had not concerned themselves greatly
with matters of personnel. The sailors, commercial agents and officials
who had carried on the foreign establishments had depended upon
the natives of the country for the ordinary necessities of life. The first
attempts made in North America assumed the possibility of using
the same system, but it soon became evident that the Indians would
not "be contented to serve those that shall with gentleness and hu-
manitie goe about to allure them," as Hakluyt had promised. Moreover, the migrants had only a scanty surplus of corn and meat and on
this store no reliance could be placed. Since it was impracticable to
transport all supplies from the British Isles, the nature of these new
outposts had to be broadened. Successful trade must involve settlement,
and settlement could not be left to chance. The transportation of
colonists became a vital part of every project of Western planting.

In this indirect way the problem of migration arose. Its solution
depended on the judgment and needs of each individual company.
When in the course of time the colony as a political body succeeded
to the rights of the colony as a trading corporation, it also inherited
the privilege of determining its own policy of immigration. Conse-
quently there never was, in the old British Empire, a consistent
imperial program of settlement. When the thirteen continental colonies declared their independence, their white inhabitants numbered

approximately two and a half millions. Though they were all referred to as "colonials," neither they nor their ancestors had a homogeneous origin. They included prudent heads of families, prisoners transported for major crimes and minor offenses, stray adventurers, military deserters, trading-company servants and bond laborers of a half-dozen different categories. Along with these there were religious sectarians who, individually or in groups, had sought a refuge. In addition, the population embraced the human residue of two rival empires that had disappeared—New Netherland and New Sweden. The history of their coming is a record of confusion that easily loses coherence in the mass of details. But out of the maze there gradually emerges a clear-cut type which was not the product of law or policy but the creation of experience—the individual who could be spared in Europe, who was needed in America: the standard immigrant of the nineteenth century.

If the Virginia and New England settlements had been started fifty years earlier, it is possible that national interest would have injected some semblance of unity into the peopling of the New World. Elizabethan England was troubled by the multitude of its inhabitants. The country roads and city streets were filled with "sturdy vagabonds." The poor had multiplied beyond any relief that private charity could extend. How was the nation to find a vent for its hungry unemployed? In answer to this question, some sought to arouse their fellow countrymen to the importance of undertakings across the sea. Let those whom old England could not support be the nucleus of a new England in America, and both the old and new would draw strength from the presence of the other.

But by 1600 the emergency had passed, and colonization as a remedy had fallen into disrepute. The transition from arable to pasture, from the raising of grain to the production of wool, was complete, and the dislocation of population occasioned by these changes had subsided. The Elizabethan poor law had provided the parishes with a social stabilizer which received credit for all the improvement that the times revealed. Moreover, schemes for the settlement of Ireland, loudly advertised as cures for overpopulation, had aroused considerable popular resentment. Thousands of families, it is true, had been established in the north and west of that island, but the Irish were hostile, and England was too close at hand. Hundreds of the settlers were massacred by their embittered neighbors, and hundreds fled back to the poverty and safety of their native parishes with stories of hardships that dampened enthusiasm for similar ventures. Only the Scots seemed to thrive. For the next century Ulster was a colony of Scotland, serving as a training school for a race of pioneers who were to perform hardier exploits beyond the Atlantic.

The Virginia plantation of 1607 began in an atmosphere still strongly tinged with the old spirit of romance. Every petty Indian chief was described as an emperor, and every squalid village as a city. But the organizers, realizing that these cities had no riches to loot, believed that whatever wealth Virginia was to yield must come from the forests and the subsurface wealth. Therefore, along with the soldiers on the first expedition, were sent artisans and miners. The terms were hard, and there was no press of people seeking passage. Even under the royal charter of 1609, seven years of service, ruled by military discipline, were required before a settler could receive a grant of land, the possibilities of which were, of course, entirely unknown. Captain John Smith, years later, recorded that it cost "many a forgotten pound to hire men to go." The disasters of the first expeditions need not be recounted. Within a few years everyone was disillusioned. No gold mines had been discovered, no passage to the Pacific had been traced. The expense of obtaining naval stores from the pine forests devoured all profit, and the Indians did not provide the market for English woolens anticipated by many of the merchant adventurers who had invested in the enterprise. All the original objects of the company had failed.

But in both London and Virginia were men who would not admit failure. If the territory could not be exploited it could be developed, and a recognition of the true nature of the country's resources created an entirely new situation as regards the plan of peopling. The regime of John Smith had begun, and his communications emphasized the need of carpenters, smiths, masons, husbandmen and "diggers up" of trees and roots. The bands sent out in 1609 suffered shipwreck and fever, and less than half reached their destination, but even the gloom engendered by such experiences did not discourage the leaders. They clung to the land and the people they possessed, and saw to it that deserters when captured were shot, hanged or broken on the wheel. Fortunately by 1616 the survivors among the first comers had served their terms of service, and with the acquisition of their own land a new spirit became apparent. Most of them, however, still considered themselves exiles and dreamed of the time when they could return to England with the profit of their labor. The authorities, no longer possessing any legal claim to their presence, adopted measures more subtle than hanging or breaking on the wheel. They began the introduction of shiploads of maidens, "whereby the Planters minds may be the faster tyed to Virginia by the bonds of Wyves and children," and thus completed the process of transforming the trading post into a settlement.

4 / WHAT IS AN AMERICAN?

Crèvecoeur's book is a classic account of early America—full of information and of praise for the land of food and freedom. Michel Guillaume Jean de Crèvecoeur (J. Hector St. John), came from Normandy to New York about 1759, and although he later returned to France, he spent almost thirty years in the American colonies and states. In 1782, as a farmer in Pennsylvania, he published his ebullient Letters from an American Farmer, of which the following is but a sample. It is a prototype of many later epistles to benighted Europeans by emigrants who—some sincerely, some for ulterior purposes—praised their New World with exuberant idealization.

. . . He is arrived on a new continent; a modern society offers itself to his contemplation, different from what he had hitherto seen. It is not composed, as in Europe, of great lords who possess every thing, and of a herd of people who have nothing. Here are no aristocratical families, no courts, no kings, no bishops, no ecclesiastical dominion, no invisible power giving to a few a very visible one; no great manufacturers employing thousands, no great refinements of luxury. The rich and the poor are not so far removed from each other as they are in Europe. Some few towns excepted, we are all tillers of the earth, from Nova Scotia to West Florida. We are a people of cultivators—scattered over an immense territory, communicating with each other by means of good roads and navigable rivers, united by the silken bands of mild government, all respecting the laws, without dreading their power, because they are equitable. We are all animated with the spirit of an industry which is unfettered and unrestrained, because each person works for himself. If he travels through our rural districts he views not the hostile castle, and the haughty mansion, contrasted with the clay built hut and miserable cabbin, where cattle and men help to keep each other warm, and dwell in meanness, smoke, and indigence. A pleasing uniformity of decent competence appears throughout our habitations. The meanest of our log-houses is a dry and comfortable habitation. Lawyer or merchant are the fairest titles our towns afford;

From J. Hector St. John [Crèvecoeur], *Letters from an American Farmer* (London, 1782), extracted from pp. 46–53, 73, 76.

that of a farmer is the only appellation of the rural inhabitants of our country. It must take some time ere he can reconcile himself to our dictionary which is but short in words of dignity, and names of honour. There, on a Sunday, he sees a congregation of respectable farmers and their wives, all clad in neat homespun, well mounted, or riding in their own humble waggons. There is not among them an esquire, saving the unlettered magistrate. There he sees a parson as simple as his flock, a farmer who does not riot on the labour of others. We have no princes, for whom we toil, starve, and bleed: we are the most perfect society now existing in the world. Here man is free as he ought to be; nor is this pleasing equality so transitory as many others are. Many ages will not see the shores of our great lakes replenished with inland nations, nor the unknown bounds of North America entirely peopled. Who can tell how far it extends? Who can tell the millions of men whom it will feed and contain? for no European foot has as yet travelled half the extent of this mighty continent!

The next wish of this traveller will be to know whence came all these people? they are a mixture of English, Scotch, Irish, French, Dutch, Germans, and Swedes. From this promiscuous breed, that race now called Americans have arisen. The eastern provinces must indeed be excepted, as being the unmixed descendants of Englishmen. I have heard many wish that they had been more intermixed also: for my part, I am no wisher, and think it much better as it has happened. . . .

What then is the American, this new man? He is either an European, or the descendant of an European, hence that strange mixture of blood, which you will find in no other country. I could point out to you a family whose grandfather was an Englishman, whose wife was Dutch, whose son married a French woman, and whose present four sons have now four wives of different nations. He is an American, who leaving behind him all his ancient prejudices and manners, receives new ones from the new mode of life he has embraced, the new government he obeys, and the new rank he holds. He becomes an American by being received in the broad lap of our great Alma Mater. Here individuals of all nations are melted into a new race of men, whose labours and posterity will one day cause great changes in the world. Americans are the western pilgrims, who are carrying along with them that great mass of arts, sciences, vigour, and industry which began long since in the east; they will finish the great circle. The Americans were once scattered all over Europe; here they are incorporated into one of the finest systems of population which will hereafter become distinct by the power of the different climates they inhabit. The American ought therefore to love this country much better than that wherein either he or his forefathers were born. Here the rewards of his industry follow with equal steps the progress of his labour; his labour is founded on the basis of nature, self-interest; can it want a stronger allurement? Wives and children, who before in vain demanded of him a morsel of bread, now, fat and frolicksome, gladly help their father to clear those fields whence exuberant crops are to arise to feed and to clothe them all; without any part being claimed, either by a despotic prince, a rich abbot, or a mighty lord. Here religion demands but little of him, a small voluntary salary to the minister, and gratitude to God; can he refuse these? The American is a new man, who acts upon new principles; he must therefore entertain new ideas, and form new opinions. From involuntary idleness, servile dependence, penury, and useless labour, he has passed to toils of a very different nature, rewarded by ample subsistence. This is an American. . . .

An European, when he first arrives, seems limited in his intentions, as well as in his views; but he very suddenly alters his scale; two hundred miles formerly appeared a very great distance, it is now but a trifle; he no sooner breathes our air than he forms schemes, and embarks in designs he never would have thought of in his own country. There the plenitude of society confines many useful ideas, and often extinguishes the most laudable schemes which here ripen into maturity. Thus Europeans become Americans.

But how is this accomplished in that croud of low, indigent people, who flock here every year from all parts of Europe? I will tell you; they no sooner arrive than they immediately feel the good effects of that plenty of provisions we possesss: they fare on our best food, and are kindly entertained; their talents, character, and peculiar industry are immediately inquired into; they find countrymen every where disseminated, let them come from whatever part of Europe. Let me select one as an epitome of the rest; he is hired, he goes to work and works moderately; instead of being employed by a haughty person, he finds himself with his equal, placed at the substantial table of the farmer, or else at an inferior one as good; his wages are high, his bed is not like that bed of sorrow on which he used to lie: if he behaves with propriety, and is faithful, he is caressed, and becomes as it were a member of the family. He begins to feel the effects of a sort of resurrection; hitherto he had not lived, but simply vegetated; he now feels himself a man.

Ye poor Europeans, ye, who sweat, and work for the great—ye, who are obliged to give so many sheaves to the church, so many to your lords, so many to your government, and have hardly any left for yourselves—ye, who only breathe the air of nature, because it cannot be withheld from you; it is here that you can conceive the possibility of those feelings I have been describing; it is here the laws of naturalization invite every one to partake of our great labours and felicity, to till unrented, untaxed lands.

5 / THE GERMAN BACKGROUND OF EMIGRATION

More soberly and more factually than Crèvecoeur, and with emphasis on the scene of emigration rather than on that of immigration, the following passage moves us into the nineteenth century. Here it is the "push" of unhappy conditions that appears stronger than the "pull" of American freedom and fertility. Germany was one of the major lands of emigrant origins. The migration therefrom, both eastward to Russia and westward to the United States, is judiciously analyzed in the monograph by Mack Walker, now professor of history at Cornell University.

Economic Factors Determining the Groups which Emigrated from Germany

The accumulation of areas in which various factors acted to produce emigration was a part of the general process of mobilization of population and productivity during the second quarter of the century. Improved transportation in the thirties, brought about by the clearing away of tolls and restrictions on the Rhine, Main, and Neckar and by the introduction of the steamboat made seaports more accessible to more interior areas and people. Besides providing cheaper and easier transportation for Auswanderer, the opening of the river routes caused economic dislocation, especially for small manufacturers and handicraftsmen. The creation of the Zollverein, the customs union, had a similar effect, destroying manmade barriers behind which the economies of particular regions had taken shape. Improved transportation and the removal of trade barriers, both designed to bring greater economic prosperity, brought to many only economic distress; the handicraftsman suffered from the advance of a liberal economy. Moreover, Germany's unfavorable world trade balance worked to encourage emigration, reaching behind the seaports into interior areas as they became accessible; it passed up the river valleys with barges which brought in overseas imports and sought paying loads for the return trip to the sea.

Between 1830 and 1845 the Auswanderung became heavy in Hessen-Darmstadt, substantial in Hessen-Kassel, and spread to Franconia, Westphalia, Hanover, and Oldenburg, thus moving northward and eastward from the 1816–17 core. Once it took hold in any area, it was unlikely to leave it, and that area usually thereafter added its regular contribution to the growing volume of the movement. From the district of Damme in Oldenburg, for example, the emigration was 17 in 1830, 28 in 1831, 99 in 1832, 260 in 1833, and only once—in 1840—fell below 100 before 1855.

The Auswanderung of 1830–45 was, with the exception of certain northern areas, decidedly a movement of what may be called the lower middle class: neither great landowners nor harvest hands, but small farmers who cultivated their own land; not apprentices, nor unskilled laborers, nor great merchants, but independent village shopkeepers and artisans; next to no one from the larger towns and cities. They were people who relied upon their own skills and wished to do so in the future, who had property that could be turned to cash; they traveled on their own resources. They were people who had something to lose, and who were losing it, squeezed out by interacting social and economic forces: a growth of population without a corresponding growth of economic bases, and the increased cosmopolitanization and liberalization of the economy.

The principal means of production was agriculture; its main capital resource was land, which permitted of little expansion. In southwestern Germany, an area of divisible inheritances, agricultural lands had been divided and subdivided to match increased intensification. The family plot decreased in size and remained marginal or submarginal in terms of its capacity to support those who depended upon it, so that in Baden, Württemberg, the Rhenish Palatinate, Rhenish Prussia, and the Hessens a large part of the landowning population stood perpetually on the verge of hunger. Increasing productivity did not keep pace with increasing population; intensification of agriculture had gone past the point of diminishing returns in western Germany, where the family-sized, noncommercial holding was the basis of the land system. As Friedrich List pointed out, with the example of his native Württemberg always before his eyes, every improvement of agricultural methods—improved fodders, the cultivation of potatoes, the establishment of agricultural credit institutions and schools—simply strengthened the trend to what he called a dwarf economy, a *Zwergwirtschaft,* of tiny marginal holdings. Marginality is the characteristic to be emphasized. The dwarfing process typically meant the establishment of a household on resources barely able to support the beginnings of a family; as the family grew in size, the land became insufficient, and any of a number of possible crises might drive the family to give up the struggle. This is one reason why the family-group Auswanderung predominated in the divided-inheritance areas of southwestern Germany, where families could be established on economic bases insufficient to sustain them. The marginal farmer might gain some cash income, or at least a lightening of his burden, by hiring out his children to larger estates. But when the harvest was poor, he lost not only his own income, but that of his children; or at least they came home. In this part of Germany, unlike America, so high a level of intensification had been reached that the greater labor potential of a large family was of no value—more children meant more mouths, not more hands.

The disproportion between land and labor caused intense competition for land, so that the real cost of land rose, sustained in some areas like Hessen by bourgeois investment and by great landowners who used their compensation from feudal dissolutions to increase their holdings. The price of land was disproportionately high to the income it produced. But the same high land prices which prevented the small farmer from acquiring enough land to feed his family made it possible for him to move it; he might be able to liquidate his inadequate holding at a price enabling him to cross the sea to America and buy a larger farm, which would absorb his and all his family's energies productively. Those unable to do so did not ordinarily emigrate. The contrast with American conditions was simple and real, as List pointed out in 1842: "The more the growth of rural population exceeds the proper proportion to the amount and productiveness of the land, the more the value of land increases while the value of labor and of man declines; while in uncultivated or thinly populated but fruitful countries the reverse relationship prevails, for there land has little or no value, and labor and man much. The Auswanderer, to use the terms of the disciples of the theory of value, transfer in their own persons a ware which is of little value to a place where it has great value."

The heavy representation of wine gardeners among the Auswanderer again emphasizes the factor of marginality. The grape is a notoriously unstable crop, which cannot be raised successfully without adequate reserves; a series of bad years always sent many growers down their valleys to America.

Closely connected with the excruciating decline of the small farmers into precariousness was the pressure on small businessmen and artisans. They relied ultimately upon a surplus of agricultural production, for which they exchanged their goods and services. If the farmer had no surplus, he could cut most of his purchases back sharply, or sometimes eliminate them. Local manufacture, notably of metal goods and textiles, suffered from the development of a transportation net, the consolidation of tariff regions, and the erection of factories. Prussian factory competition was troublesome enough in southwestern Germany; the low tariff tendencies of the Zollverein, determined by Prussian agricultural interests, made matters worse. The chorus of complaints over the surplus of artisans of all kinds grew steadily, especially after 1840. Between 1840 and 1847, one sixth of all the weavers of Württemberg went bankrupt. Carpenters, saddlers, masons, and blacksmiths found little to do, and their incomes declined.

The trend toward legal economic freedom (*Gewerbefreiheit*) probably had less to do with the excess numbers and proletarianization of the petty burghers and artisans than did the decline in demand for their services. Yet it may be that economic freedom sometimes permitted the establishment of independent shops and businesses, and families dependent upon them, on precarious bases—a *Zwergwirtschaft* like that in agriculture—wherein the family lived hand to mouth, could not apply all its energies usefully, and was too sensitive to economic and other shocks. Something of this sort may be visible in the Rhenish Palatinate, where economic freedom and a high marriage rate seem to have been related. Moreover, economic freedom was hard on the smaller and less able operators; under conditions of decline competition was harsh, and many failed, or feared they must. The shopkeepers, the artisans, and the small farmers faced similar conditions in their struggles to maintain independence: their means were too small; they had no reserves, no room for maneuver; and energy and ambition were not always enough, for there was too little room to apply them. Out of those who failed emerged in the villages a propertyless class, now without independent place and without capital: a proletariat.

Proletarians did not ordinarily emigrate, though. Proletarianization, that final failure, precluded even escape. Many wine gardeners of the Ahrtal waited too long in the late thirties and early forties; after a decade of bad vintages only a fraction of those who wished to go to America could find enough money to get them there. The unemployed or underpaid industrial workers of Saxony and Silesia seldom had a chance. The proletariat was rather another product of the process that lay in the background of the Auswanderung. It was an economic drag and was seen as a social danger; it raised the taxes which the still solvent citizen had to pay, it deprived him of customers, and it showed what might happen to him. The proletariat did not emigrate, but it drove others to do so. Even the *Heuerleute,* wage laborers of Oldenburg and Hanover, among whom Auswanderung began in the early thirties, were not proletarians; they were rather *becoming* rural proletarians, because of the enclosure of common lands, the decline of linen and other home industries, and the growth of population beyond what the rather rigid agricultural structure there could absorb.

The emigration between 1830 and 1845 probably included a higher proportion of prosperous and skilled, educated people than that of any other time, while the poorest and least valuable members of the society stayed behind. Contemporary observers never ceased to be astonished by this; to contemporary officials, this was the most dismaying aspect of the emigration, for they took cash with them and reduced the tax bases of the localities. It was declining standards for themselves and their children, rather than absolute lows, that drove them; even with a substantial holding, a family with six children might fear economic ruin, especially when the possibilities for extra work at home or nearby were disappearing, swallowed up in rural decline and the new urban industrialism. The "social problem" of the growing cities was not a directly contributing factor, for the Auswanderung came from the villages, not cities; yet it had an important effect, for the small farmer knew his sons must go to the city if his farm was to remain large enough to support a family. The prospect of joining the wage-labor class, the lowest he knew, was abhorrent to the pride, training, and traditions of the independent freeholder or artisan. Despite his difficulties and his fears, he was reluctant to move to the city; better to go to America, where his hope for success in the old ways was higher. He who chose Auswanderung might be attached to his home village, but probably not much to his home country, let alone the German Bund; if his roots must be torn up, let them be transplanted to a new land, not another province or another duchy; he was likely to think that other parts of Germany were worse off than his own. Higher income for the artisan, cheaper land for the peasant—in America the value of a man was greater than at home. In both instances, the psychological manifestation of the economic crisis was the overriding fear of decline into the proletariat, which Marx in those years noted in the lower middle class.

6 / IRISH EMIGRATION

Ireland provided the most spectacular example of emigration in the nineteenth century. The deep-seatedness of its causes and the far-reaching nature of its social and economic effects are here analyzed by Arnold Schrier, professor of history in the University of Cincinnati, who did intensive research among both the archives and the people of Ireland.

Causes of Irish Emigration

In general, four groups or classes occupied the soil of Ireland and together formed a sort of social and economic pyramid. At the top were the landlords. Of this numerically small class, one fifth (that is, less than one per cent of the total population) possessed 80 per cent of the cultivated area in 1869. Below the landlords were the leaseholders who comprised 2.5 per cent of the population, were mainly Protestant (that is, Church of Ireland), and held the land in perpetuity. Generally speaking leaseholders as a class did not engage in tillage and to a great extent were the occupiers of large grazing farms. Either under these leaseholders or directly under the landlords were usually one or more middlemen, that is, people who made their living by renting land themselves and then letting it out in smaller holdings on short leases or annual tenancies. Motivated solely by a desire for quick profits, middlemen were the most oppressive class of all and made as much money as they could at the expense of their subtenants. Under the landlords, leaseholders, and middlemen came the tenants who were the most numerous class of all and formed the broad base of the pyramid. Although some landlords and leaseholders did their own farming, it was largely on the crops raised on tenant farms that the people of Ireland lived.

There were three classes of tenants. The annual tenants, who numbered over half a million in 1870, formed 77 per cent of the occupiers of farms. This was the typical "small farmer" class that settled mainly on lands valued at less than fifteen pounds per year, lands which com-

Ireland and the American Emigration, 1850–1900 by Arnold Schrier. University of Minnesota Press, Minneapolis. © 1958 by the University of Minnesota. Pp. 11–15, 66–75.

prised more than 50 per cent of the total acreage under cultivation. Next came the cotters who lived in poor cottages usually located on somebody else's land. They had very little land of their own and generally rented a patch of conacre (that is, land let annually on an eleven-month tenure to the highest bidder) to grow a crop of potatoes or to pasture their flocks. At the very bottom of the pyramid were the agricultural laborers. They had no land at all but often they too rented a patch of conacre. In a normal season the potato crop from one acre was enough to maintain a man, his wife, and six children for three quarters of the year, albeit in a shocking state of personal squalor.

For the greater portion of the half-century the lot of all three tenant classes was one of misery and insecurity. The chief cause of this condition was found in the nature of the Irish land system, a dreary mosaic of rack rents (that is, exorbitantly high rents in relation to farm income), insecurity of tenure, and a frustrating law regarding improvements. Secure in the conviction that the demand and competition for land would never abate, landlords or their middlemen often charged exorbitant rents for the meager patches tilled by the small farmers. The peasant farmers, aware that if they could not meet the payments their landless neighbors would be ready and eager to step in and try, toiled on in desperation. There was no way to resist the extortionate demands of the landlords.

The law, moreover, discouraged farmers from attempting any improvements on the land. Legally all such improvements belonged to the landlords, not the farmers, so that when improved farms were sold the landlords were the ones who realized the profits from the enhanced value of the land, not the original improvers. Furthermore, if a farmer did effect an improvement, the landlord often took this as a sign of increasing wealth and raised the rent. . . .

For a while longer Irish farmers continued to enjoy a free market for Irish corn in Great Britain. But with the adoption of free trade by Britain just after the famine the final blow was administered. While the repeal of the corn laws acted as a boon to British industry, it began the destruction of the Irish export trade in cereals as cheap foreign food flooded the British market. To be sure, the small peasant farmer or agricultural laborer in England and Scotland also suffered from the new policy of free trade, but he at least could hope to find employment in one of the rapidly growing industrial towns in his own country. No such hope was held out to his Irish counterpart.

This theme of lack of employment runs like a constant refrain through the latter half of nineteenth-century Irish history. When asked why all his brothers and sisters emigrated to the United States in the 1880s, the unhesitating reply from an octogenarian in County Cork was "because there was no great livin' for them in Ireland." The same answer had a monotonous regularity in other counties as well.

This then was the economic background against which Irish emigration in this period must be viewed. While it was doubtless the most important element, it was not the only one in the pattern of predisposing conditions. The dynamics of rural Irish family life was also a contributory factor. Each farm was worked as a unit by a family of husband, wife, and children, and the farm was the support of all. As the children reached adulthood there was the growing realization that only one of them, usually the eldest son, would inherit the farm. Subdivision as a means of providing for the others had begun to die out by the mid-1840's . . . and after 1852 the practice almost completely disappeared.

For the younger sons and daughters, therefore, the inheriting of the farm by their eldest brother meant only one thing: they "must travel." The eldest son then married, reared a large family of his own and the cycle was again repeated. Arensberg and Kimball have described this system as one "whose very nature predisposed it to disperse population" and since there was little or no industry to keep these younger sons and daughters in the country, emigration became a "logical corollary" of this dispersal.

Emigration, however, became more than a corollary to the Irish; it became an accepted fact of life. So natural and normal did emigration seem to them that at the turn of the century the Frenchman L. Paul-Dubois considered it to be one of their customs. "Children," he declared, "are brought up with the idea of probably becoming emigrants." . . .

Effects of Emigration on the System of Irish Landholding and Land Use

In a country like Ireland, where emigration has been a perpetual phenomenon for over a century, it was inevitable that the question should arise as to whether the nation was the gainer or the loser by it. The question not only arose, but was frequently the subject of vigorous and sometimes passionate debate. It is only in recent years that rational inquiry has increasingly replaced impassioned oratory.

Foremost in any discussion of the impact of emigration on Ireland's economic structure must be the consideration of land. Many contemporaries and most newspapers of the later nineteenth century sincerely believe that with Ireland pre-eminently an agricultural country, the continued exodus from the rural areas could only have the most disastrous results for the land system. Not only were the small tenant farmers leaving en masse and thereby drastically reducing the number of small farms, it was also contended that the untilled land was being converted into pasture or worse still, being allowed to revert to waste. Emigration was draining the countryside of its agricultural laborers and leaving farmers little alternative but to convert their farms into grazing fields. Such developments were universally deplored, and it was unquestioningly assumed that a transition from tillage to pasture was necessarily detrimental to the best interests of Ireland's agrarian economy. To what extent were these fears justified and to what degree was emigration responsible for the rapidly changing pattern of Irish agriculture? To answer these questions it is necessary to look more closely at the changes wrought in the system of Irish landholding and land use.

The most dramatic transformation in the total configuration of Irish landholding occurred during the decade of the 1840s, a period also of the heavy famine emigration. In 1841 over 80 per cent of all farms in the country were concentrated in holdings of under fifteen acres; ten years later the proportion had dropped to less than 50 per cent. During that decade also the number of holdings of fifteen acres and above rose from less than 20 per cent to over 50 per cent. In effect the character of this change represented an extensive elimination of the small garden farms held by the laboring classes (usually on conacre) and a sweeping reduction of the cotter tenantry. Over the course of the following fifty years farms of under fifteen acres declined by only 17 per cent while those of over fifteen acres rose by a mere 7 per cent.

It is clear therefore that during the 1840s emigration and the alteration in the pattern of Irish landholding were closely related to one another. The nature of that relationship is not susceptible of any exact definition, and the best that can be said is that emigration was both cause and effect of the sharp decline in the number of small farms. The famine was the prime mover of that period, and many of the laborers and cotters who left did so because hunger, or the workhouse, faced them at home. Their departure meant the abandonment of the numerous small patches of ground upon which they had barely managed to eke out their subsistence.

However, this was also a period of widespread forced clearances. Irish landlords, long distressed by the uneconomic practice of excessive subdivision indulged in by their tenants, and anxious also under the impact of the repeal of the corn laws to convert their lands to pasture as rapidly as possible, saw in the calamity of the famine an opportunity to consolidate their holdings. The large-scale clearances which they carried out further swelled the emigrant flood.

The transformation wrought in land use was no less important, and in some respects more striking, than that brought about in landhold-ing. In twenty-four Poor Law unions where population declined by 27 per cent during this later period, the area ploughed diminished by 44 per cent, whereas in fourteen Poor Law unions where rural population fell by 23 per cent the area ploughed decreased by only 5 per cent. For the country as a whole it has been shown that when population was falling fast, tillage fell more than proportionately to population, and when population was falling more slowly, tillage fell less than proportionately to population.

Rural emigration, however, was not the only factor which led to the decline in tillage; economic considerations also played a part. The revolution that took place in Irish agriculture in the fifty years follow-ing the famine was in effect a transition from the production of cereals to the production of animal products, or more correctly the raising of animals. By the turn of the century Ireland had become a great breed-ing ground for livestock, especially cattle. The movement was essen-tially a rational one and developed very largely under the impulse of price stimuli.

Effect of Emigration on Irish Labor

Second in importance to the land problem is the question of labor and whether it was substantially affected by emigration. In Ireland this meant primarily agricultural labor. Here again opinion differed widely regarding the beneficial as opposed to the detrimental effects of the exodus. Those on the negative side were many. As early as 1854 one Poor Law inspector in the west of Ireland reported that despite a con-siderable diminution in the number of workmen there was very little increase in the general rate of wages for agricultural laborers. From Cork, Kerry, Limerick, and Clare that same year came reports that although wages had risen, so had the price of food, and the wage in-crease, it was said, bore little relation to the advance in price of the necessaries of life. The *Newry Examiner,* on the other hand, was con-vinced that wages would rise so high as a result of the emigration that it would upset the scale of rents and lead to the ruin of small farmers. More than a decade later the manager of several large estates in Ire-land admitted to a parliamentary committee that emigration had

raised wages but promptly informed them that in his opinion the rise
was not sufficient to affect the "wholesome condition" of the laboring
population because laborers still did not have constant and regular
employment. At the very end of the century, C. H. Oldham, looking
back over fifty years of continuous emigration, asserted that because
of it "The farmer has, today, to pay more wages for a less efficient
workman. . . ."

Adherents of the opposite view were just as numerous. John Locke,
the Rathmines pamphleteer, was convinced in 1853 that emigration
"blesses him that stays, and him that goes" because it improved those
who left and raised the wages of those who remained. The lord lieutenant of Ireland writing the following year to Lord Aberdeen, then
prime minister of England, assured him that emigration had had a
"sensible and direct effect on wages, in itself a visible source of improvement," a view concurred in several years later by the emigration
commissioners and the Poor Law commissioners. One clergyman felt
certain that the effects of emigration were of the "greatest benefit" to
the laboring classes and William Donnelly, then registrar-general, saw
in it evidence of Ireland's increasing material prosperity. Indeed, asked
one Irishman of his compatriots, if emigration has led to a rise in
wages, "why should we affect to lament what has conferred a lasting
and solid advantage on our countrymen?" Lord Dufferin, that self-
appointed spokesman for Irish landlords, positively "rejoiced" that
emigration had forced him to pay higher wages because he was "above
all things, an Irishman," and anything which strengthened the independence of the tenant farmer or added to the comforts of the laborer's
existence could not but please him.

Statistics on Irish wages are unfortunately very deficient so that a
correlation with emigration over a long period of years is not possible.
Regardless of the incomplete figures, however, there is evidence that
between 1843–44 and 1860 the wages of agricultural laborers rose by
more than 57 per cent and this, it has been maintained, was mainly
attributable to emigration. A. L. Bowley, the foremost student of the
problem, concluded that over the course of the half-century emigration
operated to the benefit of the laborers. Before 1870, he pointed out,
work was unobtainable for a great part of the year. By the middle of
the 1890's work was not only available, but wages were higher and food
cheaper. The condition of the laborer had witnessed a considerable
improvement and emigration, he felt, could take a large share of the
credit.

Emigration did more than contribute to a rise in wages. By reducing the number of laborers it had other effects as well, although not all were agreed that these were entirely beneficial. The commonest complaint was that there would not be enough laborers left to help with the planting and harvesting, and as early as 1851 there were reports of the difficulty of obtaining agricultural laborers. A generation later, according to one contemporary, it was "all but impossible" to get extra hands at harvest time in spite of increased wages. In the following decade a County Cork farmer testified that as a result of the labor shortage farmers employed no laborers at all and cultivated no more land than "their own help" (that is, family) enabled them to do, a circumstance, he stated, which forced them to keep the rest of their land in grass.

Emigration also led to a depletion in the ranks of domestic servants, and this fact was noted by the Poor Law commissioners in 1854. Some years before, Nassau Senior recorded in his journal the personal inconveniences emigration was causing one individual who complained that he could not hold on to his servants. About thirty years later the London *Times* correspondent reported from Donegal that female domestic servants were becoming "scarcer every day" because as soon as they had saved up enough money for their passage they went out to America "in search of service and husbands." Somewhat less generous was the *Tuam Herald* which felt that no sooner did young girls attain working age than away they hied to "slave and scrub and stifle in American cities."

Offsetting the inconveniences occasioned by the diminishing number of laborers and domestic servants was the fact that for those who remained there resulted a degree of regularity in employment that had seldom been known. As early as 1850 the manager of the Provincial Bank of Ireland informed the lord lieutenant that if emigration had not raised wages, it had at least made labor more steady in some districts and more abundant in others and he only wished that the state of affairs were more general. His optimism was borne out a few years later by the emigration commissioners who noted that although wages were still at a minimum, more people were receiving them and unemployment was considerably reduced. They were seconded by the Poor Law commissioners who reported that throughout Ireland there was a more continuous state of employment for male agricultural workers as well as for female domestic servants. More than a decade afterward, constancy of employment was again stressed as one of the two main advantages derived from emigration, the other being a rise in wages. By the end of the century A. L. Bowley thought the greater regularity

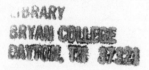

of employment a more important result even than the increase in wages.

7 / THE MENNONITES OF ALEXANDERWOHL

Massive economic causes operated in the Irish emigration and in emigration in general. But many individuals and groups migrated for very different reasons, even though economic matters might loom large in their history. The following passage concerns one of the groups most tenacious of its special beliefs and customs. The Mennonites, having strong convictions about the kind of life they wanted for themselves and their children, but lacking sufficient numbers to create a state where they could maintain their system, have had to migrate again and again. Something of the difficulties they faced, the differences of opinion among them, and their industrious persistence through repeated transplantings, is portrayed in this abstract of an article by Professor Frederick A. Norwood of Garrett Theological Seminary. Professor Norwood has made an extensive study of this subject that is soon to appear.

Among the Mennonites emigrating from the Netherlands under the pressure of religious persecution in the sixteenth century, one group was peculiar in that through four centuries and three major migrations it managed to preserve its Old Flemish religious and social heritage. A product of the internal dissension that often occurs under external pressure, this group migrated in the middle of the sixteenth century to the delta of the Vistula River in West Prussia, where they founded the village of Przechovo, which soon was to become the religious and spiritual mother village for several others in the area. Conditions were favorable for growth: the political decentralization and instability in the area afforded these Dutch Mennonites a certain protection against external control, and the land itself was similar to that of their homeland, although vast improvements in diking and damming had to be undertaken. This had once been attempted by the Teutonic Knights, but their efforts were by now all but obliterated, and it required three generations of toil and sacrifice to make the land productive again. Once established, the old Mennonite order was maintained for almost two centuries, preserving the traditional ways of worship and of farming,

Condensed from an unpublished manuscript by Frederick A. Norwood. For more complete treatment see Frederick A. Norwood, *Strangers and Exiles, A History of Religious Refugees,* in two volumes, forthcoming from the Abingdon Press.

as well as the traditional family names. Then, under the tremendous population pressure caused by their high fertility rate, the old order began to give way. As the number of marriageable relatives beyond the first-cousin mark declined, intermarriage in the wider community increased and with it came adoption of local customs, an increase in church membership and a resulting decline in discipline, and finally the adoption of German in place of Dutch as their language. Under increasing pressure of conscription and visible deterioration of the Mennonite traditions, a growing desire for a new location developed.

On the invitation of the Russian government, many Mennonites migrated to the Ukraine where they formed the Chortidtza and Molotschna settlements. The latter area was the more prosperous and better organized, and it was there that the village of Alexanderwohl was established in the early nineteenth century by a large group from the old village of Przechovo. These migrant descendants of migrants brought with them and transplanted intact the religious and social institutions of their mother village. The villages were strung out along the one street and common fields, orchards, and woodlands bordered on the outskirts. Church and school dominated the village scene, and because of a combination of government tolerance and the villages' isolated positions, local government was reserved to the villagers themselves. This later was to prove a mixed blessing, since increasing prosperity and political dissension were to cause much ill feeling and even two church schisms. Prosperity and population increase also were to cause a repetition of the by now familiar story of expansion, intermarriage, increased church membership, and decline in discipline. Among the causes of their success on the rich black-earth steppe were their remarkable aptitude for agriculture and the diligence with which they pursued it. Outstanding among their contributions were improvement in cattle stocks and the development of high-grade wheat. In spite of, or because of, their prosperity and the recurrence of the problems already mentioned, many of the orthodox Mennonites became disenchanted with the state of their society and under the pressure of land shortage (the population doubled every twenty years) they began searching for a new land where they could preserve their heritage. Since Europe no longer afforded the necessary opportunities they turned their eyes toward the other side of the Atlantic, to the new lands of Canada and the United States.

The former seemed at first glance to be more attractive, since the Canadians were less prone to find administrative difficulties in admitting them and also because they were willing to grant a more definite exemption from military service. However, the friendliness and personal attention of President U. S. Grant greatly impressed the Mennonites, and the United States came to be the main receiver of the emigrants from the Russian steppe. The group that finally settled in Kansas was one of three dissident groups from the Molotschna area. The second and largest, being the most liberal and culturally the best assimilated, remained in Russia. The third was a group of extreme conservatives that preferred the more rigorous life in Canada, where they were granted exemption from conscription. The one settling in the United States was a moderately conservative group, the Polish- and Swiss-infiltrated old West Prussian settlement in Alexanderwohl. It settled in Kansas on a large area of railroad land purchased from the Atchison, Topeka, and Santa Fe Railroad. Here they soon replaced their ugly immigrant houses with individual sod houses and later with sturdy frame dwellings. The land was rich, and they soon made rapid progress, being generally very well received by their neighbors. In turn, they gradually adopted American customs, abandoning their villages and settling on detached farms. The church remained the central and dominating force in their lives and served as a guardian of their Old Flemish traditions, but the old ways lived more obviously in the little things—the old clocks on the walls, the beautiful storage chests, and the Russian-Mennonite furnace-stoves.

Having fought for their beliefs for four centuries, their traditions had remained as symbols of their life and character, symbols protected and cherished for their own sake. Gradually, even the symbols became dormant as persecution lessened and prosperity increased. But when their peculiar ways were threatened and persecution increased, the symbols were revived, to be carried with them to new lands, seemingly never to be destroyed.

8 / THE ATLANTIC CROSSING

Many thousands of the emigrants who left hopefully from European ports never reached their transoceanic destination. Travel conditions were especially bad during the mass pressures of the nineteenth century, before governments on both sides of the Atlantic at last awoke

Edwin C. Guillet, *The Great Migration: The Atlantic Crossing by Sailing-ship Since 1770* (New York: Thomas Nelson and Sons, 1937), pp. 10–16 (passim). By permission of the author.

to the necessity of regulation and before steamship travel reduced the time spent in passage. Edwin C. Guillet of Toronto has made a thorough study of the conditions of sailing-ship traffic.

Regulation and Conditions of Immigrant Ships

The policy of laissez-faire, so characteristic of the last half of the eighteenth century, applied to conditions of ocean travel just as it long prevented the alleviation of crying abuses in industry. Emigration was sporadic, however, and the accommodations were fairly satisfactory, as there was competition for a comparatively small traffic. In the 1790's the exodus to America increased, and it was no longer necessary for masters to offer a comfortable passage. Ships became overcrowded, and an agitation to ameliorate conditions gradually gathered headway. The first government regulation, the Passenger Vessel Act of 1803, resulted largely from the investigations of the Highland Society of Scotland. It aimed to protect Highlanders from the rapacity of emigrant agents, and in its representations to Parliament gave several notable examples of the unscrupulous manner in which vessels were crowded. In 1773 a British ship of 300 tons sailed for North Carolina with 450 passengers, of whom twenty-five had no sleeping accommodation until twenty-three who had had berths died. One hundred Highlanders died on an overcrowded brig *en route* to New York in 1775. In 1791 a 270-ton emigrant ship left the Isle of Skye with 400 passengers, who were provided with most miserable accommodations. The berths were only 18 inches high and two feet wide, and they were arranged three tiers high. Two pots, each of 24 pints capacity, comprised the cooking facilities. In 1801 two ships of 550 tons carried 700 passengers each, and while ostensibly they had the usual two tiers of berths, they are believed to have erected a third after putting out to sea. On one of these ships 53 died, while the sufferings of the survivors were severe. Investigators concluded that the law regulating conditions in the transport of slaves rendered their accommodations preferable to those of many an emigrant ship.

In the regular emigrant ships there was usually a steerage about 75 feet long by 20 or 25 feet wide and 5½ high. On either side of a five-foot aisle were double rows of berths made of rough planks; and each berth, designed to accommodate six adults, was ten feet wide and five feet long. The four rows of thirteen berths might therefore hold 312 people, while the five-foot aisle was congested with their baggage, utensils and food. Occasionally passengers slept in hammocks which they supplied—if, indeed, there was any place to sling them. In the semi-darkness dozens of children played, and the confusion and noise may readily be imagined. In the fetid atmosphere the passengers often went days without ventilation. In fact in some ships the dirty bilge water of the hold seeped through the temporary flooring, while the foul-smelling cargo contributed its share to the common misery. The plight of the emigrant under conditions which continued long after the first state regulation was hardly to be avoided, and, as a contemporary points out, "Their trials were so intense that multitudes, who might have reached our shores in good health, came here worn out, impoverished and diseased, and never, in innumerable cases, recovered from the fatal consequences of unexpected impositions."

The Passenger Vessel Act of 1803 limited the number of passengers to one to every two tons of the ship's register. This was no criterion of the vessel's total passenger list, however, for there were not infrequently, in addition, almost half as many small children, those under fourteen being reckoned as half an adult, those under seven merely a third, and infants under one year not counting at all. The passengers who needed most space were denied it by this method of computation, and the large number of deaths among children was the natural result of a condition which encouraged contagious diseases. Among other regulations, the Act of 1803 called for a surgeon on each ship and sufficient provisions for all passengers. The Act brought forth loud protests from ship-owners, who immediately raised their rates.

All sorts of frauds were practiced by the unscrupulous agents and brokers who frequently bought up the entire steerage accommodation of emigrant ships. As John Campbell wrote to Lord Bathurst in 1815, "What we have chiefly in my humble apprehension to contend with are the wretched and infamous practices that have been followed by those emigration crimps whose unprincipled thirst for gain has led them to such a traffic at times not much less to be dreaded than the slave trade." Ships which had left port with a satisfactory certificate from the government inspector would proceed to some remote spot on the coast to take on many more passengers. Upon arrival they would escape trouble by avoiding the regular ports, dumping the unfortunate immigrants upon some unfrequented shore of New England, Cape Breton, or the lower St. Lawrence. Acts of Parliament might be passed, but masters when well out to sea observed the law perfunctorily, if at all. The Rev. William Bell tells how during his voyage in 1817 on the *Rothiemurchus*, Captain Watson refused to follow the provisions of the Act passed a few weeks prior to sailing, although he had taken plenty of butter, flour, and oatmeal on board to conform with its terms. When he refused to issue these supplies a passenger produced a copy of the Act, and feeling ran high. Finally a week's supply was distributed, and peace was temporarily restored; but on the following day the captain spitefully withheld the usual allowance of soup. At Mr. Bell's intervention a grudging compromise was effected. . . .

Following the relaxation in the regulations in 1817, conditions became so bad that there was strict government supervision again in 1823. The pendulum swung to the opposite extreme, and the law restricted the passengers to one to every five tons. Ships were required to carry much better provisions, enough for all passengers, and careful inspection was provided to see that they did so. A general outcry from agents and ship owners was accompanied by an increase of from £2 to £5 in the cost of passage. Conditions were greatly improved, but there was considerable point in a contemporary comment that the Act was valuable "if we wish to keep the pauper population at home, but the most irrational and absurd that can be imagined if we wish to facilitate their egress."

The Act of 1823 was amended in 1826, when Ireland was exempted from its provisions; and in the following year it was entirely repealed. The belief was general that extensive emigration was essential to provide an outlet for the ever-increasing surplus population. The Passenger Vessel Act of 1828 greatly cut down the food allowance. It was stipulated, however, that ships must carry 50 gallons of pure water and 50 pounds of bread, biscuit, oatmeal, or breadstuff for each passenger. Complaints that many an emigrant had been left at Quebec when he had contracted for a passage to Montreal led to the inclusion of a £20 penalty against masters who landed passengers without their consent at any place other than that originally arranged. The between-decks of passenger ships must be at least 5½ feet in height; but even this space was not entirely clear, for a considerable part of it was often occupied by large beams and other obstructions. Permission to carry three passengers for every four tons resulted in terrible overcrowding. In most vessels this regulation allowed a passenger for every 20½ inches of deck space—a condition hardly paralleled in slave ships. Under this legislation emigration reached a peak.

In 1831, 58,000, and in 1832, 66,000 left the British Isles for America; and in the latter year shiploads for Quebec left 36 ports in England, 18 in Scotland, and 21 in Ireland. One vessel was so crowded that, when a passenger attempted to go from one end of the ship to the other, the remaining emigrants had to crowd themselves into a dense mass, often being obliged to clamber on top of chests. Of sixteen vessels reaching Quebec between May 9th and July 15th, 1831, all had more than the law allowed, and half had more than a passenger per ton, the worst offender being the *Ulster,* from Londonderry, a vessel of 334 tons with 505 passengers. Under legislation of an earlier period such a boat would accommodate about 110 passengers, and in order to crowd in several hundred more, triple tiers of berths and false decks were common, and the miserable practice of alternate sleeping shifts in the berths not unusual; while fraudulent ages of passengers and many another evasion of the law were employed to deceive customs' agents and inspectors. . . .

In 1835–1836 an Act of the British Parliament reduced the passengers from four to three for every five tons. Otherwise accommodations had not improved. In 1836 two children were killed on one vessel when the crudely constructed bunks collapsed, and many preferred thereafter to sleep on deck. Captain Levinge crossed the Atlantic in 1835 in a sailing-ship which he describes as "a tub of a vessel, without a sailing point in her composition. . . . Water tanks, heaps of biscuits, barrels of pork and but one of rum; a pennant, an ensign, a skipper, a fat mate, and a superannuated lieutenant of the navy by way of agent, and a most inadequate crew, were put on board, and the transport was reported fit for sea." He refers to another vessel of 800 tons on which were huddled together some 700 men of the Royal or 1st Regiment.

The poor flooring of the decks was frequently a cause of trouble. Rats which swarmed up from the hold were sometimes killed by the hundreds in rat-hunts organized by crew or passengers. Because of temporary flooring, often employed for steerage quarters to facilitate the carriage of freight, washing or cleaning was forbidden, and it was a standing joke that emigrant ships could be recognized by their smell. During the ship-fever year, 1847, when there was but little pretense of passenger limitation on Irish ships bound for Quebec, many disease-infested vessels reached Canada. The *Elizabeth Grimmer* was in such a filthy state after being discharged from quarantine that "persons could not be had to near her, for the purpose of throwing out the ballast, for three weeks, and then even tempted only by extraordinary wages."

Legislation in 1842 had attempted to remedy such conditions by insisting upon 1½ inch floors, but it did not require the use of water in the steerage—merely dry scrubbing, "holy-stoning," or scraping. Bedding was to be aired on deck twice a week, weather permitting, and the ship was to be fumigated with vinegar at the same intervals. Passengers were ordered to clean themselves regularly on the upper deck (whether also by dry scrubbing is not indicated!) and they were urged to bear in mind that their arrival in America in high spirits or in ill health depended largely upon their attention to these rules. Until the Act of 1847 the only ventilation in the steerage of many ships was obtained through the hatchways, and these, during storms, were sometimes kept closed for a week or more at a time. The combination of darkness, foul air and illness produced a condition of misery hard to imagine. One family describes that for two weeks the steerage passengers were shut out from the light, with fever raging among them.

Not until the Act of 1847 was there any regulation that "adult passengers of different sexes, unless husband and wife, shall be separately berthed." A man on the *Julius Macgregor* in 1842 noted that "there was no separation for the sexes; yet it is surprising how soon myself and all the other passengers, the females included, became reconciled to it." The matter of segregation appears to have been left to the official emigration agent at the port of embarkation; or failing that, to the master of the ship. . . .

9 / PROBLEMS OF ADJUSTMENT

Oscar Handlin, professor of history in Harvard University, has probably done more than any other writer to dramatize the poignant personal problems of the immigrant, and these brief bits from his classic The Uprooted *give samples that bring these problems vividly before us. Conditions in the cities could be almost as deplorable as the situation aboard the emigrant ships.*

The crossing in all its phases was a harsh and brutal filter. On land in Europe, in the port of embarkation, on the ocean, in the port of arrival, and on land in America, it introduced a decisive range of selective factors that operated to let through only a few of those who left the Old World. In part these factors were physical; the hardier survived the dangers and the difficulties, the weaker and more dependent fell by the side. In part, however, these factors were more than physical, for they measured also the power of adaptation: only those who were capable of adjusting from peasant ways to the needs of new conditions

From *The Uprooted* by Oscar Handlin, by permission of Atlantic-Little, Brown and Co. Copyright 1951, by Oscar Handlin. Pp. 61–62, 146–148, 151–153.

and new challenges were able to absorb the successive shocks of migration.

For the crossing involved a startling reversal of roles, a radical shift in attitudes. The qualities that were desirable in the good peasant were not those conducive to success in the transition. Neighborliness, obedience, respect, and status were valueless among the masses that struggled for space on the way. They succeeded who put aside the old preconceptions, pushed in, and took care of themselves. This experience would certainly bring into question the validity of the old standards of conduct, of the old guides to action.

Perhaps that was the most luminous lesson of the crossing, that a totally new kind of life lay ahead. Therein was the significance of the unwillingness of the peasants to undertake the journey in the old traditional communal units. Despite the risks entailed, they preferred to act as individuals, each for himself. Somehow they had been convinced that the village way which had been inadequate to save them at home would certainly prove inadequate away from home.

Not that they derived much joy or comfort from the conviction. In any case they suffered. The separation itself had been hard. The peasants had been cut off from homes and villages, homes and villages which were not simply places, but communities in which was deeply enmeshed a whole pattern of life. They had left the familiar fields and hills, the cemetery in which their fathers rested, the church, the people, the animals, the trees they had known as the intimate context of their being.

Thus uprooted, they found themselves in a prolonged state of crisis —crisis in the sense that they were, and remained, unsettled. For weeks, and often for months, they were in suspense between the old and the new, literally in transit. Every adjustment was temporary and therefore in its nature bore the seeds of maladjustment, for the conditions to which the immigrants were adjusting were strange and ever changing.

As a result they reached their new homes exhausted—worn out physically by lack of rest, by poor food, by the constant strain of close, cramped quarters, worn out emotionally by the succession of new situations that had crowded in upon them. At the end was only the dead weariness of an excess of novel sensations.

Yet once arrived, the immigrants would not take time to recuperate. They would face instead the immediate, pressing necessity of finding a livelihood and of adjusting to conditions that were still more novel, unimaginably so. They would find then that the crossing had left its mark, had significantly affected their capacity to cope with the problems of the New World they faced. . . .

The immigrants find their first homes in quarters the old occupants no longer desire. As business grows, the commercial center of each city begins to blight the neighboring residential districts. The well-to-do are no longer willing to live in close proximity to the bustle of warehouses and offices; yet that same proximity sets a high value on real estate. To spend money on the repair or upkeep of houses in such areas is only wasteful; for they will soon be torn down to make way for commercial buildings. The simplest, most profitable use is to divide the old mansions into tiny lodgings. The rent on each unit will be low; but the aggregate of those sums will, without substantial investment or risk, return larger dividends than any other present use of the property.

Such accommodations have additional attractions for the immigrants. They are close to the familiar region of the docks and they are within walking distance of the places where labor is hired; precious carfare will be saved by living here. In every American city some such district of first settlement receives the newcomers.

Not that much is done to welcome them. The carpenters hammer shut connecting doors and build rude partitions up across the halls; middle-class homes thus become laborers'—only not one to a family, but shared among many. What's more, behind the original structures are grassy yards where children once had run about at play. There is to be no room for games now. Sheds and shanties, hurriedly thrown up, provide living space; and if a stable is there, so much the better: that too can be turned to account. In 1850 already in New York some seven thousand households are finding shelter in such rear buildings. By this time too ingenuity has uncovered still other resources: fifteen hundred cellars also do service as homes.

If these conversions are effected without much regard for the convenience of the ultimate occupants, they nevertheless have substantial advantages. The carpenter aims to do the job as expeditiously as possible; he has not the time to contrive the most thorough use of space; and waste square feet leave luxurious corners. There are limits to the potentialities for crowding in such quarters.

There were no such limits when enterprising contractors set to work devising edifices more suitable for the reception of these residents. As the population continued to grow, and the demand with it, perspicacious owners of real estate saw profit in the demolition of the old houses and the construction, between narrow alleys, of compact barracks that made complete use of every inch of earth.

Where once had been Mayor Delavall's orchard, Cherry Street in New York ran its few blocks to the East River shipyards. At Number 36, in 1853, stood Gotham Court, one of the better barrack buildings. Five stories in height, it stretched back one hundred and fifty feet from the street, between two tight alleys (one nine, the other seven feet wide). Onto the more spacious alley opened twelve doors through each of which passed the ten families that lived within, two to each floor in identical two-room apartments (one room, 9 × 14; one bedroom, 9 × 6). Here without interior plumbing or heat were the homes of five hundred people. Ten years later, there were some improvements: for the service of the community, a row of privies in the basement, flushed occasionally by Croton water. But by then there were more than eight hundred dwellers in the structure, which indeed continued in use till the very end of the century.

That these conditions were not then reckoned outlandish was shown in the model workmen's home put up by philanthropic New Yorkers at Elizabeth and Mott Street. Each suite in this six-story structure had three rooms; but the rooms were smaller (4 × 11, 8 × 7, and 8 × 7). There were gas lights in the halls; but the water closets were in sheds in the alleys. And well over half the rooms had no windows at all. . . .

Well, they were not ones to choose, who had lived in the thatched peasant huts of home. Nor was it unbearably offensive to reside in the least pleasant parts of the city, in Chicago over against the slaughter-houses, in Boston hemmed in by the docks and markets of the North End, in New York against the murky river traffic of the East Side. Such disadvantages they could survive. The hardship came in more subtle adjustments demanded of them.

Certainly the flats were small and overcrowded. In no room of the dumbbell tenement could you pace off more than eleven feet; and the reforming architects of 1900 still thought of chambers no larger than those of Gotham Court. In addition, the apartments shrank still further when shared by more than one family or when they sheltered lodgers, as did more than half those in New York at the end of the century. But that was not the worst of it.

Here is a woman. In the Old Country she had lived much of her life, done most of her work, outdoors. In America, the flat confines her. She divides up her domain by calico sheets hung on ropes, tries to make a place for her people and possessions. But there is no place and she has not room to turn about. It is true, everything is in poor repair, the rain comes through the ceilings, the wind blows dirt through the cracks in the wall. But she does not even know how to go about restoring order, establishing cleanliness. She breaks her back to exterminate the proliferating vermin. What does she get? A dozen lice behind the collar.

The very simplest tasks become complex and disorganizing. Every day there is a family to feed. Assume she knows how to shop, and can manage the unfamiliar coal stove or gas range. But what does one do with rubbish who has never known the meaning of waste? It is not really so important to walk down the long flight of narrow stairs each time there are some scraps to be disposed of. The windows offer an easier alternative. After all, the obnoxious wooden garbage boxes that adorn the littered fronts of the houses expose their contents unashamed through split sides and, rarely emptied, themselves become the nests of boldly foraging rodents.

The filthy streets are seldom cleaned; the municipality is not particularly solicitous of these, the poorest quarters of the city. The alleys are altogether passed by and the larger thoroughfares receive only occasionally the services of the scavenger. The inaccessible alleys and rear yards are never touched and, to be sure, are redolent of the fact. In the hot summer months the stench of rotting things will mark these places and the stained snow of winter will not conceal what lies beneath. Here and there an unwitting newcomer tries the disastrous experiment of keeping a goat, adds thereby to the distinctive flavor of his neighborhood.

It was the same in every other encounter with the new life. Conveniences not missed in the villages became sore necessities in the city; although often the immigrants did not know their lack till dear experience taught them. Of what value were sunlight and fresh air on the farm? But how measure their worth for those who lived in the three hundred and fifty thousand dark interior rooms of New York in 1900!

There was the rude matter of what Americans called sanitation. Some of the earliest buildings had had no privies at all; the residents had been expected to accommodate themselves elsewhere as best they could. Tenements from midcentury onward had generally water closets in the yards and alleys, no great comfort to the occupants of the fifth and sixth floors. The newest structures had two toilets to each floor; but these were open to the custom of all comers, charged to the care of none, and left to the neglect of all. If in winter the pipes froze in unheated hallways and the clogged contents overflowed, weeks would go by before some dilatory repairman set matters right. Months thereafter a telling odor hung along the narrow hallways.

What of it? The filth was inescapable. In these districts where the need was greatest, the sewerage systems were primitive and ineffectual. Open drains were long common; in Boston one such, for years, tumbled down the slope of Jacob's Ladder in the South Cove; and in Chicago the jocosely named Bubbly Creek wended its noisome way aboveground until well into the twentieth century.

With the water supply there had always been trouble at home too: poor wells, shallow, and inconveniently situated. The inconvenience here was not unexpected. Still it was a burden to carry full tubs and jugs from the taps in the alley up the steep stairs. Not till late was city water directly connected with the toilets; it was later still to reach the kitchen sink; and bathrooms had not yet put in an appearance in these quarters. Then, too, the consequences were more painful: city dirt was harder to scrub away, and there was no nearby creek. It could well be, as they came to say, that a man got a good bath only twice in his life: from midwife and undertaker.

10 / THE TREE THAT BARELY LEAFS

A plaintive and psychologically revealing note was struck also by some of the immigrants themselves, as illustrated in the poem "The tree that barely leafs." It was written by a workman with the word-power of a poet—Arthur Landfors, from northern Sweden.

> I took a birch, that grew in the woods,
> And planted it beside my house.
> There it was nourished, and it got good light,
> And all the care it could want.
> And every spring it came out in leaf.
> But never did it gain vigor
> Like other trees in forest and field.
> Half green it stood there, half withered,
> Its trunk was scraggy and distressed.
>
> We came here from the old world,
> When we were pulled up and torn loose
> From the earth that fostered us,
> From the milieu, from the culture

The title poem in *Träd som bara grönska* (Stockholm, 1962), translated along with the original in *The Swedish Pioneer Historical Quarterly,* Oct. 1965, p. 213. By permission of the author.

That once had given us birth.
Here we found a place in the sun,
But seldom did our roots go
Deep enough down in the soil
To take from it the strength it can give.
However fertile the place may be
We remain but stunted plants.

11 / THE UNITED STATES AND ITALY:
MIGRATION AND REPATRIATION

*From the ancient provinces of southern Italy, long plagued by malaria,
illiteracy, and resultant poverty, vast masses of peasants flocked to
America. Despite the voyages of Columbus and Amerigo Vespucci the
migratory surge was slow to develop, but in the last two decades of the
nineteenth century a million Italians sailed for America, and three
million more in the first two decades of the twentieth century. Farms
were left without workers, and villages without people. Yet the ideal
of the average emigrant was to fill his pockets with American dollars
and return to buy a house or a farm or at least to die in his native
land. Hundreds of thousands of them did so, and Italy was faced with
a returnee problem as well as with an emigrant problem.*

*George R. Gilkey, professor of history in Wisconsin State University,
LaCrosse, has investigated this phenomenon, not only by talking with
"Americani" in the taverns of Italy, but also by assiduously studying
the literature and the archives. He here poignantly describes the Italians' recognition of the problem and also their failure to meet it mean-
ingfully.*

America not only drew many peasants from their homes but she sent
back many of them—some only to visit but thousands to start life
anew in the regions of their childhood. Repatriates from other lands
went back to Italy but not in numbers equal to those from the North
American republic. During the first two decades of the twentieth century the back-flow was very large. For example, of the repatriates to
the Campania (Naples) 86 per cent returned from the United States.
For all of southern Italy and Sicily, 75 out of every 100 repatriates
returned from the United States. In central Italy 65 out of every 100

From George R. Gilkey, "The United States and Italy: Migration and Repatriation," *The Journal of Developing Areas,* II (1967), 23–35. By permission of Western
Illinois University.

returnees sailed from the Federal Union. Owing to the more permanent character of the overseas migrations from northern Italy, repatriation to that region was much less. The total returning to all of Italy from the United States between 1902, when such figures were first compiled, and the march on Rome was about 1,900,000. Additional thousands returned during the halcyon days of Fascism.

Repatriates and their remittances and savings figured prominently in the altered land-holding system and the shift of cultures that took place in pre-Fascist Italy. The countryside of many a region received a face-lifting from the repatriates. Returnees exhibited new attitudes toward the traditional social organization of their native land. Such changes prompted the chairman of the parliamentary committee investigating the conditions of the southern peasantry prior to World War I to write:

> Christopher Columbus thought he had found India and discovered America. We went forth in our own humble way to determine whether by legislative action we could alter the relations between landowners and peasants, and we found America.

This America found by the investigators was the result of the acquisition of money in the new world. Of the estimated two billion dollars remitted to Italy between 1901 and 1923, for example, 80 per cent derived from the United States. Stories of individual wealth made in America varied. But the peasantry could prove to their satisfaction that in America one lived well, ate regularly, and saved money. And they knew that in the desolate wastes of the Basilicata and the inhospitable lands of Aspromonte that was not so. Some of them who had been to America emphasized the difference. Replying to senatorial investigators in 1908, Giuseppe Chiaravallotti said:

> It is not true that the peasant who goes to America works more than at home, he works less, and is paid more. Here I make two *lire;* there I made ten. In America I ate meat every day. . . . I would rather be in America than have a hundred pieces of land here.

There were stories of good luck but also examples of less fortunate persons. Giovanni Locchino of Nicastro twice traveled to Pittsburgh, taking home 2,500 *lire* from his visits. A home of his own took one-half of his hard-earned money. For a living he returned to work the land again. Benevento Carmine of Tricarico learned the trade of watchmaking during a ten-year stay in New York. He claimed he had saved

20,000 *lire* of which 10,000 remained after he paid his debts. Two doctors of Lagonegro painted an even rosier picture of neighboring *americani*. They told investigators in 1907:

> Here there is a small American bourgeoisie, repatriates from America who receive three or four *lire* a day from public investments. There are over one hundred families who live this way without doing a thing.

The literature of emigration speaks often of the higher living standards, new homes, and land proprietorship all made possible through remittances. And in many instances American money also gave artisans and small merchants the means to establish new businesses or to expand old enterprises as illustrated in the picturesque seaside village of Sorrento.

The repatriates' age-old dream for land ownership in some areas sent prices spiraling upward. Choice bottom lands tripled in value within a very short time, such as in the Abruzzi where prices rose to $2,100 an acre, and in Calabria where they went up to $920 an acre. Near Caserta returnees paid up to $1,650 an acre for irrigated lands. In the southern provinces whole sections of mountain lands were purchased by *americani*. In those regions less desirable plots brought as low as $20 or $25 an acre.

In addition to the purchase of land or instead of it repatriates built or purchased homes. Sometimes these new, usually larger houses were built in the native towns, sometimes in entirely new sections on the outskirts. New homes often were two-story structures with plenty of windows for light and air, and more notable still, a stall in back for pigs, donkeys, and chickens which previously had lived in some homes under the same roof and sometimes in the same room with the family. Whole quarters of so-called "American homes" were built in the southern provinces.

The American experience showed in transformed community life where many aspects of economic and social life carried the imprint of material gains and changed social attitudes. The parliamentary report on Calabria noted that the *americano,* unlike the gentleman farmer of the old order, cultivated his own lands. And repatriates who had lived away from home no longer showed the traditional respect for the hereditary gentry. America entered the social struggle between the defenders of the old order and the peasants. Dollars gave to the repatriates the means to invade the ranks of the landowners and to claim for themselves the amenities belonging to that class. The intellectual uplift accompanying the economic improvement set the *americani* apart from their nonemigrant neighbors frequently. Wrote a student of the south:

> With the money, the emigrants bring with them a spirit of very accentuated independence which, although not concrete or convergent toward any specific attribute, is manifested in the slightest act in the life of the *americani*. . . . They flaunt their superiority in dress, in spending, in work, in language.

As a person, the peasant had changed radically, another commentator noted:

> If you observed the emigrant at his first departure and see him again after some time of residence in America and especially in North America, you will find him *unrecognizable*.
> Above all the exterior appearance is infinitely different: before, he was covered with filthy rags, was careless about personal cleanliness, and was possessed of an air of uncertainty, confusion, and suspicion; now you see him changed into a civil, self-possessed, loquacious person. Dressed well, sometimes stylishly, he often has a new suit, a gold chain, a ring, and other ornaments, and endowed completely with good manners, he speaks with whomever is near without suspicion, recounting his American adventures from beginning to end.

Americani also became joiners; they flocked to the mutual aid workers' associations, joining mainly for the sake of belonging, not for the small financial benefits. With a consciousness of a common experience which set them apart, they developed a sort of *esprit de corps*. They formed new peasant leagues or joined old ones of which they took charge.

The ebb and flow of the migrant tide brought varied reactions from among the upper classes and the students of the movement and its impact. To the eulogies such as those of Gino Arias there were bitter responses from other quarters. Observers deplored the loss of labor, the breakup of families owing to the absence of the father, and the social dislocations due to the great shift of people. Writers bitterly scored the treatment of the Italian in America.

Critics reserved much of their denunciation for the repatriation of their fellow countrymen. They protested at the spectacle of the repatriate who came home with money which he spent in a profligate manner, who refused to tip his hat to his old *signore,* and who sought to enter the ranks of the bourgeoisie, aspiration to which by tradition he was not entitled and for which he was not qualified in their opinion. Calabrese "Americans" were accused of shirking the responsibilities of community political life; their only concern, it was said, was to have a full pocket book and a satiated stomach. Returnees to the Abruzzi, it was observed, exhausted by giving the best years of their lives to the American industrial machine, posed a difficult problem for their native land which was ill prepared to provide for them in their debilitated condition. They brought back alcoholism, tuberculosis, and other diseases to the solitary hills and with those a spirit of discontent and restlessness. After a time of exposure to America there were those among the repatriates who were disappointed in their home towns of which they had dreamed so much while working abroad. The charge of *retrogradismo* or backwardness was levelled at the home community by Abruzzi Americans. At the same time they exalted the "land of liberty" for its lack of pettyfogging officials and outdated customs. Bernardy was saddened to hear the words, "Git up, Charlie, git up," echoing in the Abruzzi hills as a repatriate from Pennsylvania admonished his donkey on the road to Palena, or as she observed two peasant women comparing shoes, the one proudly displaying a pair from Red Granite, Michigan, for "a dollar ninety-eight, guaranteed." These were in her words "symptoms of the American fever" that had sickened the folk of the Abruzzi.

The practice of drinking "hard" liquor brought reprobation on migrants from the United States. In Calabria, *americani* befuddled by brandy settled their quarrels "in the American manner . . ." by using their fists instead of the traditional knife. Further, the repatriates were censured as a highly unstable element in Italian society. Many regarded the homeland as a place for a vacation, their return a sentimental journey. They were lazy, wasteful, uncooperative individuals who did nothing to improve their lands or promote agricultural progress, according to their detractors. The *cafoni* of the Campania, a Neapolitan landlord complained, had learned nothing of value in America; and on their return home they sank back into the old ways of living. "An American peasant, as the returned emigrant is called here," he wrote in 1906, "is not distinguished from the others except for long trousers instead of the short ones that they all wore before." Elsewhere the voice of disapproval took a different turn. Once the gentlemen of the old social order had been pompous and proud. "Sometimes now," wrote an observer of Lucania in 1907, "the pride of the *americani* is almost intolerable; they have become annoying in their turn."

In the face of these and other denunciations of the migrations, many distinguished men came to the support of the peasant who sought to rise from his lowly place in life by labor in America. Among those who emphasized the benefits were Pasquale Villari, Luigi Bodio, Angelo Mosso, and Giovanni Lorenzoni. These and others argued that emigration had given many of Italy's forgotten little people economic and intellectual uplift impossible to achieve at home. The concern of these men centered on the class of small peasant-proprietors which the processes of emigration had in some instances created and in others encouraged. The growth in numbers of independent small owners and the strengthening and increase of agrarian leagues and cooperatives seemed to point the way toward significant improvements in agrarian Italy.

It was Villari's view that to accept the momentary changes which emigration brought was not sufficient. He wrote in support of a proposal by Di San Giuliano to set up small properties in Sicily by means of a system similar to the American homestead scheme. And he added:

> It is certain that the economic change brought by emigration could be the beginning of a true social regeneration, creating small property and the independent peasant proprietor. But it would be necessary not to leave everything, as we do, to chance. It is not enough to create small property if at the same time we do not defend it from the dangers that threaten its existence: its division, pulverization, and absorption by large property. That the small proprietors have the capital and the necessary knowledge to cultivate well is required.

To prevent what happened so often—the purchase by returned emigrants who bought land at high prices only to lose it when their money was gone, Villari proposed that an institute be formed to aid those repatriates. He would call it the "Public Institute for the Acquisition of Small Property in Favor of Returnees from Emigration." And Lorenzoni looked forward to the breakup of large estates in Sicily with the hope that a rural middle class might grow from among the peasantry.

Senator Luigi Luzzatti supported the Villari plan, and in the immediate post-World War I years, others pleaded for government action and reform. Michelangelo Trombetta asked that credit be provided for small owners and urged the establishment of the homestead system to form and conserve small properties. His plan required the expropriation of some *latifundia* for public use and the reform of local administration, policing, taxes, and utilities. Franchetti had planned to buy a *latifundium*, divide it into small farms, build houses and barns on these farms, and sell them to returnees from emigration. But the

Emigration Council of the national government did not favor the plan nor would it lend money to the Baron for his project.

In 1920 a further investigation into land ownership indicated that a million proprietors had been added to the rolls since the census of 1911. However, most of the holdings were quite small and of little use either for the maintenance of the family or for the national economy. Agricultural statistics for 1927 indicated that 87 percent of the farm owners held only 13 percent of the land while .5 percent of the owners held 42 percent of the rural properties. Nor did statistics confirm the Fascists' claims that they were "deproletarizing" Italian agriculture. Within the ten-year period between 1921 and 1931, farmers who owned lands they cultivated decreased by nearly one-half million and rental and sharecropping tenants rose by almost 400,000. Domination of the southern agrarian areas of Italy by the great estates continued into the post-World War II period. And because at least for the time being emigration cannot be depended upon to solve the "southern problem," Italy has had to turn to other means to develop these backward regions.

The migratory movement, then, was an effort by the southern Italian peasants to solve their economic and social problems. The American dream was most often a peasant dream. Precisely because this was so, the effects on the Italian nation as a whole were limited in scope. Emigration was a palliative, not a solution for the economic and social woes of Italy. Whatever the cultural effects, they were indirect; no purposeful action, no visions of a brighter future planted and nourished them on the Italian scene. Mostly these effects came to Italy willy-nilly by individual carrier—the repatriate. The *americani*, the immediate bearers of the culture-impact, were almost entirely persons of little education and meager background, devoid of knowledge about the world outside their immediate surroundings. Their villages, their families, their friends, and the myth of America which appeared more enticing than ever when they returned home, made up their world. Without the help of their own country that world would always remain small. Even the wealth and prestige gained by immigration to America was not enough to make them in one generation the political and cultural leaders of a proud and historic nation. Ultimately the most numerous successful emigrants were those who did not return to Italy but who helped to build America.

12 / THE M-FACTOR IN AMERICAN HISTORY

George W. Pierson, professor of history in Yale University, is one of the most articulate interpreters of migration into America and within America. Here he turns his attention, quite appropriately, to the fundamental factor of mobility (the M-factor) as a characteristic of the American scene and of the American people. And although his treatment is applied to the United States, it obviously applies elsewhere as well. This selection is condensed from a paper given at a conference on American culture, in Munich in June, 1961.

My basic proposition is obvious: Movement means change. To transfer is in some part to transform. *"Wanderung meint wandlung,"* as the Germans put it. And all forms of movement, from mass exodus to simple milling around, have shared in this subtle process of alteration.

Why should motion cause change? First, because *institutions* do not move easily. A few will be destroyed; many more are damaged; nearly all are shaken, and have to be pruned, simplified, or otherwise adjusted to survive the transplanting. To a degree *displacement* means *replacement* of institutions.

Why again should migration cause modification? Because the migrants are not average people. As a group they do not represent a fair cross section of the society they are leaving; as individuals they tend toward exaggerations of one sort or another; as settlers they won't wish to reproduce the society they have left, or succeed in reproducing it even should they so desire.

This brings us to the third great reason for change, the new circumstances: that is, the hardships and accidents of the crossing, the strangers encountered on the road, the unaccustomed climate and geography of their new environment. Movement means exposure, and successive exposures compel unexpected changes.

It may be urged that more credit should go to the strangers and the new countries. Or it may be observed that migrations are often the result or the symptom of changes that have already taken place in the parent society. And with both these ideas I agree. On the one hand, many immigrants were Americanized only long after they got over. On

George W. Pierson, "The M-Factor in American History," *American Quarterly*, Summer Supplement, 1962. Copyright 1962 by the Trustees of the University of Pennsylvania. Condensed from pages 275–289, and reprinted by permission of the author and *American Quarterly*.

the other, not a few American types, like the puritan and the business-man, had already appeared in sixteenth-century Europe. So migration served both as prologue and as epilogue; it has been the means of change and the effect of change (as well as the cause). Yet no move-ment of people or institutions, however started or motivated, can take place without further alterations. For migration selects special types for moving; it subjects them to exceptional strains on the journey; and it then compels them to rebuild, with liberty to choose or refuse from the mail-order catalogue of Western experience. On top of all that, repeated movements, such as we in our country have known, seem to have a cumulative, or progressive, effect.

What parts of a civilization, what elements in a society, does the M-Factor attack? Apparently, all parts. Before his death Ellsworth Huntington, who was one of the earliest American scientists to become curious about this phenomenon, came to see in migration a selective force so strong that it affected the stock and temperament of a people as well as its culture. After some hesitations, I believe we will concur. For I believe it can be demonstrated that movement changes the physical population, the institutions and group structures, the social habits and traditions, the personal character and attitudes of the migrants.

Allow me to offer some random, familiar illustrations at this point.

The American population? It was formed and re-formed by migra-tion. To begin with we were all immigrants. Moreover, because the Atlantic was open, people from many lands and nations came to these shores, until we were the leading conglomerate of the West, a Rainbow Division of Europe. Political scientists call us a pluralistic society. Sociologists find culture conflicts endemic.

Again because the migrants did not all come at once, but in inter-mittent surges, and because in free movements the later comers, as strangers, are handicapped and must enter the lower levels of their class and occupation, the natives or earlier-comers have repeatedly found themselves pushed upstairs, to the more skilled jobs, to the managerial posts, to the position of employers and capitalists. At the same time, moving upstairs was difficult, so difficult that the older stock felt it had to cut down on the number of its own children, if it was to grad-uate them into the higher levels of living—so difficult that the next-to-last comers tended to resent the labor competition of the newcomers and tried to exclude them. Thus the Yankees industrialized with the aid of other people's children. Meanwhile these laboring generations, as they matured, tried to keep the jobs for themselves and, whether as skilled artisans or later trade union bosses, as Know-Nothings in the 1850s or McCarthyites a century later, became the strongest champions of immigration restriction, the most suspicious of new foreigners, the uncompromising 100 percenters. So from 1820 to 1920 what ought to have been for the Anglo-American population a series of European additions became instead a progressive physical substitution. And after 1920 the freedom to immigrate was shut off by the votes of the very groups which had benefited from it earlier. But why did not and has not this stepladder movement of infiltration produced a stratified, hierarchical, skyscraper society? The answer is again the M-Factor, but this time internal migration. Inside, the freedom to move remained, and a man could get out of his cellar in town by building a one-story cabin up country, or he could come off his eroded acres into Chicago, where the rising buildings and professions had elevators in them.

If we now turn from questions of nationality and occupation to the age and sex characteristics of our population, we find that here, too, the M-Factor has left deep marks. For three hundred years, or at least until the great depression, we were a young country. We boasted of it. Foreigners rarely failed to mention the childlike innocence, the boyish enthusiasm, the youthful drive and bustle and activity-for-activity's sake of these strange Americans. The youth of America, quipped Oscar Wilde, is its oldest tradition. And perhaps we were guilty of a certain "shortage of adults." At least the demographers have proved that our Constitution was made for adolescents—as late as 1820 the median age of the population was only 16 years, and it was not until well into the twentieth century that that median soared above 25. That is, it was only after preventive medicine had started to prolong the lives of the infirm, and immigration restriction had cut down on the annual influx of bachelors and young marrieds, that we first really began to feel middle-aged. How does the M-Factor figure in this? Well, students of migration have rediscovered the fact that it is overwhelmingly the young, between the ages of 15 and 25, who move—and in the first waves or pioneer phases, it is primarily the young men. The frontiers, whether of farm or factory, start emphatically male (*Oh Susannah, don't you cry for me!*).

Yet the men were not to have it all their own way, for the M-Factor can give things a sardonic twist. Migration has perennially represented rebellion against past tyrannies or authorities, against the father no less than against the lord or priest, against the husband no less than against the father. Thus, after the first settlements had been established, the open spaces and open opportunities of this country just invited the younger generation to leave home and strike out on their own, and the able young men accepted the invitation. Even today it is the rare son of ability who does not insist on leaving the town where he was born to try to make his way in a larger world. Meanwhile the pioneer women, being scarce as well as weak, found that they had inadvertently acquired a scarcity value. For them, as well as for the children, migration meant progressive emancipation—an emancipation eventually crowned by woman suffrage, Mother's Day and much symbolic statuary. Thus, as our lonely forefathers pushed relentlessly westward, and the idea of equality came galloping up behind, the Pioneer Mother replaced the Pilgrim Father on the sculptor's pedestal in the town square. (Whether the statuesque Miss America has now replaced her bronzed mother in the popular imagination I leave to braver men to say—we may note only the querulous complaints of our English and Continental friends that we are today a woman-run and child-dominated subcivilization.)

If we next pursue the M-Factor from our population to our economy, what will we find? An economy in which transportation has loomed extraordinarily large—witness the railroads, the automobile age and the airplane industry of today—witness also in our myths how prairie schooners and pony express, paddle wheelers and the long whistle of the trains, Ford cars and the Spirit of St. Louis have entered into the folklore of our people.

> The wheels are singing on the railroad track
> If you go, you can't come back.
> Hear the whistle blow.

For Americans, it has been said, the automobile restates a national principle, since, after all, the settler was the first auto-mobile. In the U.S. a mile is something to put behind you. Where else would you find a place named Stillwater Junction?

More soberly, if our interest runs rather to our religious peculiarities, it might be observed that the need for settlers, and the ease of exit and entrance from one colony to the other, made toleration and disestablishment of churches almost inevitable from the start.

Let us now proceed to ask, on a more systematic basis, how, just how, have migration and movement acted to convert Europeans into something rich and strange?

Considering the matter first on a broad social scale, I would propose that the M-Factor has been (turn by turn or even all at once): (1) the great Eliminator; (2) the persistent Distorter; (3) an arch-Conservator; (4) an almost irresistible Disintegrator or Atomizer; (5) a heart Stimulant or Energizer; and (6) the prime source of Optimism in the American atmosphere, a never-failing ozone of hope. Also, (7) the Secularizer and Externalizer of our beliefs, and (8) the Equalizer and Democratizer of social classes. Indeed a little reflection will suggest still other ways in which migration has shaken its European ingredients into new patterns.

Migration was the great Eliminator? Nothing could be plainer. In theory you can't take everything with you when you move. Some goods are too bulky or delicate to be put on ship; some household possessions will fall out of the covered wagon. Again, in a free migration, not all elements in a society will wish to move; the dregs will be too spiritless and impoverished to emigrate unaided; the ruling classes entirely too successful and satisfied. A student of mine once maintained that settlement transferred the accent from *nobility* to *ability*. Considering the transfer culturally, however, one must recognize a tragic impoverishment. Despite all our gains of goodness or plenty or freedom, the men of the highest attainments and greatest skills had stayed home—and with them their arts and refinements, their leisure-class culture. Like war or fire or inflation, migration has been a great destroyer of inherited treasure.

On top of this, the M-Factor has promoted distortion in an even more drastic way. For moving forces the reclassification of values. Why? Because the land of destination attracts more strongly for one or two presumed goods than for the others (as for economic opportunity perhaps, or political freedom, or the right to worship in one's own way). So if a family is to go, they have to believe, or persuade themselves, that the particular goods to be realized are more important to them than all the other social goods, which may be diminished, or left behind altogether. By elimination and wilful distortion a moving people becomes a narrower society: thinner and shallower, yet in some things much more intense.

This calls attention to a third and almost paradoxical characteristic of migration: its conservatism. People moved to save as well as to improve. But when they found they couldn't take everything with them, then a curious thing often happened. They came to value even more highly what they had succeeded in preserving. Having suffered such privations, having sacrificed so many other possessions, they clung to what was saved with a fiercer passion. Witness the Puritans with their wilderness Zion, the Mormons under Brigham Young, or even Turner's leapfrogging pioneers. For these last, as for so many others, it had become easier to move than to change their vocation, their habits, their antiquated methods. Migration, I would suggest, could be a way of promoting change—and of avoiding it, too. Flight can be an escape from the future as well as from the past.

The M-Factor, we must next realize, was an almost irresistible Disintegrator or Atomizer. Few authoritarian institutions from Europe could stand the strain of Atlantic distances or the explosion of American space. So either they decentralized or died. Witness the early church. In Virginia the episcopal organization proved so little suited to the far-flung tobacco plantations that the Church of England almost withered away, whereas in New England the Puritan branch of the same church developed a localized or Congregational organization, and flourished.

In our expanding settlements the arm of the State (like the authority of the bishops) shriveled, and a kind of physical individualism sprouted. On the trail, society tended to break down into chance parties of moving families or individuals. And at the destination everything was to be reconstructed. It took energy and courage to move, and more energy to make the move succeed. Hence migration was a great stimulus to action—and when such action repeatedly succeeded (or, as we may say, "worked"), then perhaps the beginnings of a habit of action had been established, both for oneself and for one's neighbor. The American reputation for activism, as for self-help and neighborly helpfulness, surely needs no underlining.

Migration was not only the Destroyer, Distorter, Conservator, Atomizer and Energizer of western society, but its most effective "Optimizer." First of all, out of the welter of old-world classes and temperaments it selected the up-and-coming and the hopeful. Pessimists didn't bother; you had to be an optimist to move.

I hope I may be forgiven if I now pass over the secularizing and externalizing influences of mobility (which Sorokin has explored) in favor of its equalitarian and leveling effects. Here the theoretical argument would be that the M-Factors are often democratic in their consequences, first because for the lower classes emigration means *"getting out from under,"* the first step on the road up; secondly because the hardships of the journey are no respecters of birth (witness the miserable failure of the early "Gentlemen" of the Jamestown Colony in Virginia). In the third place, and most significantly, the process of resettlement is a process of making new mixtures, out of a gathering of strangers, each without authority, credentials, reputation or other priority than that of arrival. In a new community (frontier or town) family and past performance hardly count. Everyone has to make his own mark, and stands equal with his fellow-strangers. The social competition, as it were, starts over, with all the camaraderie and "gamesmanship" of a new catch-as-catch-can. Migration has been a great Mixmaster. And mixtures of anonymous elements are necessarily more democratic, at least at first. . . .

Finally, because migration appealed for diverse reasons especially to extremists—to saints and real sinners, to fundamentalists and free thinkers, to dreamers and "tough bastards," to groupists and individualists side by side—our society has never received its fair share of balanced, equable, middle-of-the-road temperaments, but has been shot through with violent contradictions. Hence so many of our seeming inconsistencies, to this very day.

To me the migrant seems not a single or a simple character, but is he not recognizably different—and American?

Paradoxically, if we turn up the other side of the coin, there are the Europeans, fearful of becoming Americanized. Is this entirely out of weakness, or envy, or admiration? Hardly. Let us rather take note of a curious and unappreciated development. In the last generation mobility has swept the continent. With their *vacances payés,* their *campings,* their folkwagons, our cousins have found a new freedom. So, if today there is Americanization in Europe, and if our ways of life seem to be coming closer together, may it not be in part because the Old World societies are as never before in movement, and because Siegfried's "homo sapiens," too, is taking to the roads?

II / LATIN AMERICAN MIGRATION

Migration into Central and South America in the modern period has been in many ways similar to the migration into North America. The migration into Latin America originated largely in Europe, with a considerable influx, also, of Negro slaves from Africa. The Christian religion and European languages have come with the European immigrants and have spread throughout the southern continent. European patterns of government have been introduced, and in general, European culture has come to dominate the area.

But the differences between developments in the two continents have been perhaps more striking than the similarities. In Latin America, although there are large regions of German colonization, the overwhelming majority of immigrants have come from southern Europe. The predominant Christian influence to the south has been Roman Catholic rather than Protestant. The languages to which the newcomers have adapted themselves are Spanish and Portuguese, and the basic political institutions have been Mediterranean rather than English. A significant factor has been that after the first amazing wealth of gold and silver, the natural resources for industrial development have been less abundant in the southern continent than in the northern. Probably most important of all has been the fact that the ancient culture and population of the south proved far stronger than those forces in the north; this led in Mexico and in the southern hemisphere to more of a blending of peoples and cultures, whereas in both Canada and the United States the European heritage was overwhelming. For a brilliant analysis of the fusion of diverse cultural heritages—especially the European Christian with the Indian—see F. S. C. Northrop's chapter on "The Rich Culture of Mexico" in his *The Meeting of East and West* (New York, 1946).

And not all of the modern immigration has come from Europe. Although only a few facets of migration can be illustrated here, it must not be forgotten that in addition to the large forced migration from Africa, significant numbers of Chinese and Japanese came to Peru as contract laborers in the guano industry and in railway building, to say nothing of other groups such as the Japanese in Brazil, the Ryukyuans in Bolivia, the Okinawans and others.

Furthermore, migrational currents flowed not only into Latin America from east and west, but also in various directions within the two-continent area. In the north the interchange between Canada and the United States has been lively; in the south the major movement has been from Mexico into the agricultural lands and the cities of her northern neighborhood, and also from Cuba and Puerto Rico in the same direction. The following selections only sample this total involved complex.

13 / PEOPLING THE PAMPA

Mark Jefferson, writing for the American Geographical Society, produces a striking illustration of the effect of political conditions upon immigration, with Argentina as the scene of action.

In the 1850s the Argentine government encouraged the establishment of semicommunal agricultural colonies. In addition to his general study Mr. Jefferson made a survey of the twentieth-century condition of the first of these colonies—Esperanza (Hope). Some 2,000 Germans, Swiss, and French settled there before 1870, and by 1930 the population had grown to about 9,000, and the city was flourishing. The Germans, particularly, long maintained their own language, clubs, and school, but during World War I there was remarkably little friction in the community. Intermarriage and a common enterprise had slowly welded the group together, and in the twentieth century almost all, no matter how blond, were speaking Spanish and calling themselves Argentinians.

Little Immigration at First

From the independence of 1810 to 1854, when Urquiza became president, the Argentine Confederation grew very little: there was no immigration of significance and nothing like general agriculture. As a mat-

Mark Jefferson, *Peopling the Argentine Pampa*, American Geographical Society Research Series No. 16 (New York: Am. Geog. Soc., 1930), pp. 41–49. Reprinted by permission of the American Geographical Society of New York.

ter of fact Buenos Aires city is known to have received only 700 foreigners in the forty years from 1770 to 1810. Before independence there
was practically no immigration, because the Spaniards did not allow
it. Even natives of Spain had to get a difficult special license to come
to America.

At independence, immigration was at once proclaimed to be the
great and pressing need of the country; but it did not come for nearly
fifty years, because those were years of anarchy and tyranny. The
Spanish habit of excluding Creoles from any share in government had
kept them unfit to govern. The patriots who governed the United
States under the Revolution and under the Constitution had usually
governed first under England. Government was no novelty to them,
but the men who undertook to guide the first steps of the new-born
Argentine Confederation were mere theorists at governing, men full of
excellent schemes which did not work. They wanted immigration and
did not know how to get it. And they were city Creoles. Behind them
were the Pampa and the upland provinces; in both, the gaucho.

Agriculture Developed Only as Result
of Later Large Immigration

The thing that was fundamental in the gaucho character was his familiar use of horses and cows. He might be poor or he might be rich;
he might be white or he might have a considerable strain of Indian
blood; he might be subservient to a patron or he might enforce homage
as a landowner or even as an outlaw—a *gaucho malo*—but he could
not very well live much in town. His interests were dead set against
town interests. Agriculture was a town affair carried on in those days
in the outskirts of the cities, as is market gardening—the intensest
form of all agriculture—the world over. Those 373 square miles of
tilled land are proof of it. Now that 4,700,000 immigrants have come,
there are nearly 100,000 square miles of cultivated land. And these
immigrants brought it under tillage. See how the allowance of tilled
land per capita of the population has increased through the last half
century.

	1865	1873	1888	1895	1900	1905	1910	1914
Acres per capita	0.13	0.7	1.9	3.0	3.7	5.6	7.0	7.7

This looks large beside 0.9 in Italy and Germany, 1.5 in France, 1.7
in Russia, 2.0 in Rumania, and 2.2 in Denmark, though 4.8 in the

United States and 6.0 in Canada are more like Argentine figures.

Texas might well have been expected to have a cattle-hunting period like the Argentine when plowed land was almost nonexistent, but the figures do not let us believe it. However, the great agricultural states of North and South Dakota, taken as a unit, show most surprising figures.

	1860	1870	1880	1890	1900	1910	1920
Acres per capita	0.4	3.1	8.5	21.5	29.0	31.3	33.3

The two states had more than 19 acres per capita in cereals alone in 1919 and show a high use of the land. The Territory La Pampa, which the Argentines call their Far West, in 1914 had 26 acres in cereals to each inhabitant, 44 acres of cultivated land, though 15 acres of this, in alfalfa, is very likely really pastoral land.

In every case, however, the amount of Argentine tilled land in 1865 turns out to be extremely small. It appears that nowhere in the world is there a land that has been colonized from Europe for three hundred years and still had to wait the arrival of newer Europeans to begin any effective use of its soil.

Rosas' Contribution in Breaking Power of Gaucho Chieftains

The independence of the gaucho, especially when he owned land, made him slow to accept the authority of the town theorists in the place of the Spanish authorities whom he had helped so materially to overthrow. Rather he tended to gather power into his own hands and to seek to extend it. Each such gaucho if forceful tended to become one of the *caudillos,* or petty chieftains, who loomed so large in the period of anarchy that followed the Revolution.

It was the great contribution of Rosas to the Republic, selfish and bloodthirsty tyrant though he was, that he so completely broke up and destroyed the power of the numerous *caudillos* who infested the country. His epoch (1830–1852) was one when country was put above city, anarchy above law, barbaric force above civilized society, and— since civilization appeared to come from Europe—all Creole things above the things of Europe. It was an epoch when thousands of decent citizens could save their lives only by flight and exile. As a logical part of this program immigration was forbidden and all intercourse with foreigners discouraged.

How Roca Brought Prosperity

Quite as striking as the prevention of immigration by the epoch of anarchy was its stimulation half a century later in the two terms of General Roca, who completed Rosas' campaigns of the thirties against the Indians in western Buenos Aires Province by their destruction or capture in 1870, finally opening up the Pampa to the railroad that was to make its wide occupation possible. It is the irony of history that Rosas, idol of all the most brutal elements of Creole barbarism, came from cultured Buenos Aires, and Roca, the support and stabilizer of civilization on the Pampa, came from the old-Creole province of Tucumán.

Before Roca the greatest immigration in any year was 48,000 in 1873. His first term began with 27,000 and raised it to 81,000 and two years after the end of the administration (1889) the first high point of 219,000 was reached. His second term began with an annual immigration of 67,000 in 1898 and saw it rise to 126,000 in 1904. In another two years the second high point was reached, 253,000. This latter wave of immigration continued with minor fluctuations until the World War, rising to a maximum of 323,000 in 1912. The two waves . . . comprise together the mass of the modern immigration to the country.

Are we going too far in associating the greater part of the remaking of the Argentine by immigration with General Roca? Was it not perhaps chance that it came along in his time? The net immigration to the Republic before Roca first became president was over 173,000. These men were already eagerly at work developing the long neglected treasures of the Argentine soil. Almost every individual of them was in touch with the home country, reporting his progress by sending money back. The remittances spoke more eloquently than any letters. If they were large the distant son was prospering, if they diminished or failed he was faring ill. Ignorant and illiterate as the immigrants have usually been, the clearest word that passed to Europe was not the written word but that spoken by the constant stream of those who went back and the fact of their return. Remittances were balanced against numbers of emigrants returned. Few students realize the importance of the return currents that tend to offset the streams of immigrants even to countries like the United States. There came to the United States in the year ending June 30, 1912, a total of 1,017,155 aliens. This is usually regarded as a million added to our population in that year. But it is also reported that 615,292 aliens left our shores during the same year, the net result being an addition of 401,863 persons. Our government has kept this record only since July 1, 1907. The Argentine government has kept it systematically since 1870. . . . [Between 1885 and 1912 the majority of immigrants to Argentina remained, although there were some reverse trends, as around 1890—ED. See below.]

It is certain that the would-be immigrant in Europe estimates very accurately the prosperity of the New World colonies, despite his extreme general ignorance. There was at hand a rich, virgin soil, and it was the clear intention of the Argentine authorities to open it up to the 173,000 immigrants who had stayed; these were the "colonists" at work upon it. What was needed to send back to Europe the word that should expand the streams of immigrants? Mainly stability—stability in politics, stability in currency, stability in markets. This General Roca gave them. His two six-year terms were without revolution, and that cannot be said of any other administration up to that of Roque Sáenz Peña in 1911. Roca was strong in command of his army, and under him the country was assured of peace. That is of immense significance.

You are trying to establish a farm with inadequate resources in a foreign land, whose very language you do not well understand. An officer comes along with his squad to commandeer your horses, your grain, or your own service. What can you do? You are helpless. Immigration is at once checked at the source in distant Europe. But suddenly General Roca takes office, and you have peace and security. You work long hours and your family works and the harvest comes and you remit and Europe knows that all is well. Then the immigrant stream begins to swell. There is no propaganda for immigration like the prosperity of the immigrant. Roca gave them peace and security that meant prosperity. . . . The constitution allowed him six years, and he could not succeed himself. He and Juárez Celmán had married sisters. Juárez Celmán became president; there was good hope and peace continued and there were good harvests and the word went back to Europe. Always large remittances and few returning emigrants. The immigrant stream flowed stronger and stronger—till revolution came. . . . But Juárez Celmán was not a strong man. He could not maintain peace, nor could his successors. When Roca came back again the paper peso was fixed, in 1899, at forty-four gold centavos, with machinery for keeping it there; but until then there was revolution after revolution and the net immigration was very small indeed. At the time when things came to a head and Juárez Celmán was put out in 1890, the country lost more people than it gained.

What happened at the time of the World War was entirely different.

Business was not good. The market was disrupted; ships were not to be had; and, most serious of all, men were not allowed to leave Europe but were called to the war. . . .

14 / IMMIGRANTS AND THEIR ASSIMILATION IN BRAZIL

Conditions of assimilation in Brazil illustrate both similarities and differences when compared with those in Argentina (#13). Emílio Willems of the University of São Paulo and of Vanderbilt University introduces his article with a discussion (omitted here) of two opposing attitudes: (1) total absorption of minorities into the host culture and (2) the maintenance of cultural autonomy by each subgroup. He comments upon the situation in São Paulo, where diverse immigrant elements met in an established social structure and amalgamated readily with the natives and with each other. He then turns his attention to the three southernmost provinces of the country, where German and Italian and Polish immigrants were directed into the uninhabited forest regions of the mountains, developing their own distinctive cultures there in relative isolation. But gradually, through the agency of internal migration and modernization, assimilation proceeded among these groups also:

The processes of urbanization and industrialization which had been extremely slow in the nineteenth century became more rapid during the first decade of the twentieth century and received a new and probably decisive impulse during and after World War I, when foreign competition was temporarily eliminated. Between 1920 and 1939 important industrial centers such as Joinville, Blumenau, Brusque, Novo Hamburgo, and São Leopoldo already could successfully resist European industrial competition. World War II disclosed new and unprecedented perspectives for industrial expansion.

In relation to assimilation, the importance of this process can hardly be overestimated, chiefly because the formerly homogeneous areas lost their cultural imperviousness. Brazilians of different ethnic origins now found possibilities of earning a livelihood which did not exist under the rural conditions which had prevailed since the beginning of foreign

Condensed from Emílio Willems, "Immigrants and Their Assimilation in Brazil," in *Brazil, Portrait of Half a Continent*, edited by T. Lynn Smith and Alexander Marchant. New York: Dryden Press, 1951. Pages 215–224. Used by permission of T. Lynn Smith and John van Dyke Saunders.

colonization. Professional people, merchants, officeholders, and a rapidly growing number of unskilled workers of ethnic origins other than the predominant one moved to the urban centers where they soon had opportunities of establishing control over important sections of local associational life. Labor unions, religious associations, clubs, and political parties have been increasingly influenced by newcomers whose ways of life contrasted sharply with those of the local population.

The boy of German or Italian descent became accustomed to the cultural milieu of such metropolitan centers as Pôrto Alegre, São Paulo, and Rio de Janeiro, which were so strikingly different from his provincial town that at least a partial assimilation became inevitable. The well-known conflict between generations of different cultural backgrounds invaded many immigrant homes. No matter how strong the resistance of the older generation might be, assimilation could not be stopped, and soon mixed marriages were occurring at a rate that would have been unthinkable at the beginning of the century. Before and during World War I, German-Brazilians such as Felipe Schmidt, Lauro Müller, Adolpho Konder, and others held outstanding political and administrative positions.

Although in São Paulo no segregation comparable to that which occurred in the South separated the immigrants from the native population, industrialization and urbanization affected deeply the assimilation process. In this state the foundation of urban centers may not be attributed to any single immigrant group, yet the rapid growth of new cities and the development of older ones were to a considerable extent the work of immigrants and their descendants. Between 1827 and 1939 immigration to the state of São Paulo was as follows:

Italians	945,963
Portuguese	425,546
Spaniards	387,117
Japanese	186,769
Austrians	38,122
Other nationalities	317,747
Nationality unknown	138,226
Total	2,439,490

Large-scale immigration began only in 1885—that is, at a time when the process of urbanization of São Paulo was already much more advanced than in the South. This meant that a relatively large number of immigrants could get a living in urban centers. In the state capital, for example, an Italian quarter and, later on, Syrian and Japanese "towns" developed with all the specialized functions that ordinarily are to be found in such urban zones. The Italian quarter as a distinct area has already disappeared, and at the present time this diluting process may be observed also in the Syrian and Japanese quarters. No exact data are available on the migration of immigrants and their descendants from rural to urban areas, but there are clear indications that some of these movements must have been important. In certain areas, such as the Paraíba Valley, the rapid decline of a flourishing coffee agriculture displaced many families of Italian origin from the plantations to the cities of the valley. In Taubaté, for example, many of the Italian names which appeared on the pay rolls of old coffee farms are the same as those of the families who today are the wealthiest ones in the city. It is obvious that the "superior" urban civilization with its strong attractions was likely to produce a more rapid and complete assimilation than the "inferior" rural culture. The participation of immigrants in the process of industrialization may be demonstrated by a sample taken from the statistical yearbook of São Paulo. Out of 714 industrial enterprises of various sizes, 521 were owned by immigrants or descendants of immigrants, as the names of the proprietors clearly showed.

Important changes also occurred among the immigrant families who remained in the rural areas. Many of them rose from the status of farm laborers to that of independent farmers. In some regions this change was associated with the breaking up of large estates into smaller holdings which could be acquired at low cost by the immigrants who were interested in gaining their economic independence. This meant the dispersion of cultural groups which formerly clung together in plantation villages. Integrated in different ecological and social systems, they found it more difficult to preserve Old World traits.

However, this study would be unduly one-sided if vertical social mobility was not included in our analysis. At the beginning of the immigration period the rural settlers had a social status not much different from that of slaves. In São Paulo, as has already been stated, immigration was fostered by the government and the big landowners when the supply of slaves commenced to be hard to obtain and expensive. Even in the South, where the immigrants became independent farmers, their status was not much above that traditionally assigned to slaves. In a slavocratic society, which lacks a strong middle class, manual labor is always identified with slave labor, so that the immigrants who cultivated the soil with their own hands could hardly escape the contempt of the superior native class whose social status was based upon the ownership of large estates and slaves.

Thus, from the very beginning of foreign colonization in Brazil the immigrants were struggling for social recognition and a higher status. To the extent that the settlers managed to raise their standard of living and acquired economic power, they represented an emerging middle class in a rural society in which a small upper class contrasted sharply with the large lower class of landless peons and ex-slaves.

As long as the first two or three generations formed a culturally homogenous rural society, the double rôle of their elite underwent little perceptible change. Yet social stratification among the immigrants and their descendants increased and became more rapid as their society became industrialized and urbanized. The shifting of interests of the upper class from the local to the regional or national ecological order has already been mentioned. Upper-class people became aware that the maintenance or achievement of high status and the exertion of political or economic control were becoming increasingly dependent upon the larger society rather than the local community. Thus conditions favoring a more complete assimilation emerged. They were forces which could not be entirely controlled, since institutions such as high schools, colleges, universities, and political parties were far more absorptive than had been generally realized by upper-class people.

In addition it must be kept in mind that urbanization and industrialization did not contribute solely to the benefit of the immigrants and their society. The Luso-Brazilians also played an important rôle in this general cultural change, and the members of their upper class could compete successfully in many places with upper-class people of German and Italian origin. In many cases wealth happened to be the connecting link between families which otherwise would have kept apart. Thus marriages between upper-class families, irrespective of ethnic origin and earlier prejudices, have been more frequent in the last few decades, especially in larger cities such as Pôrto Alegre and Curitiba.

Similar effects may be observed among the rapidly growing working class. Industrial wages exert a strong attraction upon the rural populations irrespective of their ethnic or national origin. Between the two world wars a social stratum of wage earners emerged wherein class solidarity and class struggle became far more important than the preservation of traditional cultural values. From the standpoint of assimilation two factors which accelerated the growth of the new labor class should be taken into account: cultural homogeneity brought about by low wages plus residential propinquity and identical educational opportunities, on the one hand, and the formation of trade unions supported and controlled by the government, on the other hand.

Thus common values and interests helped link together people of quite different cultural background. Social and racial barriers were rapidly overcome, and mixed marriages occurred much more frequently than in the other strata of this new industrial society. The fact that almost all the new industrial workers came from rural cultures deserves special attention since some of these rural cultures preserve cultural elements of recent European origin. Their bearers appear to be anxious to get rid of them as soon as contact with urban civilization has been established. A good example is furnished by the German and Italian dialects spoken by many rural-urban migrants. These dialects come to symbolize the undervalued or even despised rural culture, whereas the Portuguese language is considered urban and therefore "superior." Thus it is not surprising that the language, together with other cultural elements of rural ("inferior") origin, is quickly abandoned.

There is little doubt that, so far as urban society is concerned, traditional values brought over by immigrants and preserved by their descendants found their greatest stronghold in the middle class. Confined to local interests and closely integrated into the parish and the rather flourishing associational life of the community, the members of this class found little reward in substituting new values for the traditional ones. Assimilation was not a matter of prestige and of economic or political interest, at least not so much as in the other strata of the community. Whereas the lower and upper classes have been the more active elements of change, the middle class plays a more passive rôle. On the one hand, middle-class people cling to traditional values; but on the other hand, adjustments must be made to changing conditions which are beyond their control. Thus, for example, very few families may be found whose members do not have a fair command of the Portuguese language; but inside their homes they may prefer their traditional dialect. Intermarriages are less common than in other classes, and the family structure preserves the distinct traits of the German, Italian, or Polish kinship group.

In addition, it may be said that among German-Brazilian Protestants the attachment to Old World traits is much stronger than among Catholics. The German language has been consciously preserved in school and church because it is Luther's tongue and therefore a sacred one. "Evangelic belief and Germanism constituted, from the time of Luther, an intimate union which cannot be broken down without prejudice. . . . The German Evangelical Church of Brazil can accomplish its task only if it will be, consciously, a German National Church. Only recently, under the pressure of a rigorously conducted "assimilation policy," does this situation seem to have undergone changes, at least superficial ones.

There has been much spatial and social mobility among the immigrants of São Paulo. Thousands of families of recent Italian or Iberian descent moved from the big estates to other rural areas where small ownership prevailed, or to the cities where jobs in the emerging industries were readily available. These movements led "upwards" to landownership, to commercial or industrial jobs, and in many cases also to professional activities. Struggle for status has been fought out first along economic lines, but sometimes social recognition was not accorded even to wealthy families of recent European descent. However, in order to achieve a better understanding of this question, the state of São Paulo should be divided into the "old zones" characterized by a "traditional" society of estate owners and a landless rural proletariat, and the "new zones" where extremely heterogeneous peoples of various origins constitute a typical frontier society.

It is obvious that in the new zones national and racial origins of people could hardly play an important rôle. Many opportunities for rising in the social scale were given, and wealth soon came to be the most important criterion of status. It is in these areas that immigrants —and especially their descendants—rapidly acquire the social recognition which seems necessary for the achievement of full cultural participation and in order to induce them to abandon the distinctive cultural traits which formerly set the immigrants and their descendants apart.

In the "old zones," however, the situation was different, and in some instances the social ambitions of those of immigrant descent face a distinct challenge. In Tietê, for example, a *município* which is situated in the "old" coffee-growing central area of the state, a great part of the population is the offspring of Italians. In the nineteenth century there arose a native rural "aristocracy" of big coffee planters who cling tenaciously to family pedigrees and constitute, even today, a kind of endogamous caste to which persons lacking a recognized genealogy rarely are admitted. The Italians held a status similar to that of the landless peons and slaves. In the last 40 years, however, many Italians have risen from rural laborers to landowners, merchants, and small manufacturers; yet despite their economic position, upper-class status has been denied to them. The "traditional" families and the fashionable clubs of the "elite" have not cared to have Italians among their members. Until the end of the twenties the *municipio* was ruled by an upper-class oligarchy, and politics ran "smoothly" without opposition. On the whole, Italians did not participate in political activities, and their ballots were not "asked." In 1928, however, an opposition party arose and its leaders "discovered" the Italians who had never been registered as voters. This new "electoral mine," as it was called, was actively exploited, and soon politics came to be one of the most effective channels of social mobility. Well-to-do families of Italian descent improved their status through political participation. This does not mean that they already enjoy a position of social equality with the old native "aristocracy" but that the social and cultural gap between the two segments of the community is decreasing. In the elections of 1947 the "traditional" families once again managed to inflict a defeat upon the *Italianada,* as they depreciatingly call the elements of Italian descent.

In addition it must be stressed that the Italians found an unexpected ally in the rapid decline of coffee growing, a fact that reduced and sometimes destroyed the financial resources of the old upper class.

The whole process may be interpreted in terms of competition and conflict between the decadent old upper class and a new middle class in rapid ascension, whose distinctive cultural background has been gradually abandoned as cultural participation increased and common ideals and interests tended to fuse the population into a homogeneous whole.

From this general picture the Japanese immigrants differ to some extent, as already has been pointed out. That Japanese immigration to Brazil is quite recent has often been overlooked. It began only in 1908, when immigration from European countries was already declining, and reached its apex after 1930 when European immigration had almost entirely ceased. Of the 186,769 Japanese who entered São Paulo, 101,666 came after 1930, 57,164 between 1920 and 1930, and only 27,939 arrived prior to 1920. Of course, the Japanese culture differs much more from the native one than any European culture and therefore assimilation requires more time. In addition, the immigration from this *Eastern* empire occurred at a time when a growing nationalism bound the Japanese immigrants closely to their homeland. Yet quite contrary to what some too-hasty observers have asserted, the

Japanese could not isolate themselves, as the Germans and others were compelled to do in the South. No matter how stubbornly they tried to concentrate, everywhere they constituted only small minorities in the *municipios* in which they were established. Even within these *municipios* they are far from completely isolated.

The difficulties which are delaying the assimilation of the Japanese arise not so much from organized defense of their traditional culture as from certain features of the social structure in which they live. This structure is rural, and in it the Japanese occupy a higher level than the native *caboclos*, who are usually the only segment of Brazilian society with whom continuous contact may be established. Now the "lower" culture of this native class hardly exerts any attraction upon the Japanese with their "superior" equipment, racial pride, and deep-rooted prejudices.

Still another factor counteracts, at least partially, those conditions which are obviously unfavorable to assimilation. Japanese colonization has been mainly a cooperative enterprise in previously selected areas where commercial agriculture could be practiced profitably. Thus there was an urgent need for learning the language of the country, its business practices, and its legal system—certainly an achievement which seldom could be accomplished by the older generation. It must not be forgotten that the Japanese immigrants, though they can read and write their own language, are functionally illiterate in Brazil as in other Euro-American countries. This deficiency must be overcome at any price, and therefore it seems quite understandable that all possible efforts and even sacrifices are made in order to bestow upon the children an education that eases competition within the native society. Thus one of the most remarkable traits of the Japanese settlers is their unusual interest in schools and educational improvements. So against the wishes of the older generation or in accordance with them the public school comes to be an effective means of assimilation, especially on the secondary and higher levels, which bring the young Brazilians of Japanese descent in close contact with Brazilian urban civilization.

At the present time, the increasing spatial and social mobility of the Japanese leads to more numerous contacts with Brazilians and manifold participation in community affairs. In the last municipal elections the first representative of Japanese descent was elected in the state capital of São Paulo, together with a considerable number of deputies of Italian and Syrian extraction. The lack of racial discrimination obviously plays an important rôle in the assimilation of the Japanese.

On the whole it seems beyond doubt that assimilation is proceeding at a rapidly increasing rate. It is going on faster in São Paulo than in the deep South, where it depends on the disintegration of the whole social structure which the immigrants built up during the last century. Everywhere assimilation is connected with social mobility, industrialization, urbanization, and the emergence of sharply differentiated social classes. There are, of course, many isolated rural communities all over the southern states whose integration into national life will probably require several generations, since communication and educational opportunities are still precarious. There are residual groups, too, who offer organized resistance to assimilation, and it is not surprising that they are to be found among those immigrants who are bearers of the most divergent sociocultural heritage. But resistance ideologies, such as the cultural federalism of some German-Brazilians, are losing ground with each new generation. A more active assimilation policy and the rapid economic development of southern Brazil are factors which have played a rôle of increasing importance in recent times. Brazil's international position is now different from what it was before World War I, and this rising of the national status coincided with the political decline or defeat of almost all of the original countries from which the immigrants have come. These deep changes in international political equilibrium have certainly exerted a strong influence upon many Brazilians of recent European or Asiatic origin, who are discovering now a self-gratifying significance in being Brazilian citizens.

15 / NEW PATTERNS

Professor Anthony T. Bouscaren has surveyed the problems and the variety of opinions with regard to immigration to various countries of Latin America, in an article that illustrates the complexities and the combination of circumstances that are necessary to make immigration successful. His material refers entirely to the contemporary scene.

The Empty Spaces

Latin America encompasses 16 per cent of the world's inhabitable land area, but only about 6 per cent of the world's people. Except for Africa and Australia it has a lower density than any other major region. Vast empty spaces exist in the Amazon Valley, the plains of Argentina, the unworked forests of Southern Chile, the Llano country,

Anthony Trawick Bouscaren, "Latin America in International Migrations," *R.E.M.P. Bulletin,* Vol. 10, No. 4 (December, 1962), pp. 109–113. Reprinted by permission of *R.E.M.P. Bulletin.*

and the Guiana highlands of Venezuela. Thus, in the opinion of many, Latin America offers a vast potential for the millions of Europeans either uprooted or living in overpopulated regions. According to Kingsley Davis, this view, popular inside as well as outside Latin America, is not so much wrong as naive: "It jumps from a demographic fact to a social conclusion. There is no doubt that Latin America's physical capacity to absorb immigrants under certain conditions could be realized. But there is grave doubt that the proper conditions will come to pass. Briefly, it can be said that Latin America cannot attract the kind of immigrants it wants and does not want the kind it can attract." Indeed, some demographers hold that Latin America does not need any mass immigration at all, and that because of a population growth that, in the long run, it cannot absorb, Latin America may even become an area of emigration.

The economy of Latin America is in the same state of development as the United States in the 1870's, showing a general weakness in industry. But all the indications are that the Latin American economy will not develop in the same way or with the same rapidity as has that of the United States. Among these indicators is that mature industrialized areas are today more numerous than in the 1870's, and that new ones are more widespread; that more Latin American governments discourage the entry of foreign capital investment; and also that the world movements of goods and peoples is today more controlled. Most significant of all, the old regions from which industrial immigrants were drawn in the past—first Northwestern Europe and then Southern and Eastern Europe—can no longer furnish immigrants in great abundance because their rate of population growth has declined markedly. Countries faced with potentially declining populations are often unwilling to allow their citizens to emigrate. The relatively few surplus laborers available for migration from European countries will be in demand either within Europe itself (Western Europe is generally today faced with a shortage of skilled workers) or in other industrial areas (e.g., the dominions) that promise higher returns than Latin America offers.

The main common denominator of all Latin American countries is a considerable and still increasing surplus of unskilled manual manpower; at the same time, there exists a marked shortage of semiskilled and skilled workers and technicians. The scarcity in the upper strata of the labor pyramid seriously hampers accelerated industrialization, especially because most of the new large-scale industries in Latin America have installed highly mechanized and, in some instances, even automated plant equipment. This unexpectedly early impact of the contemporary technological revolution on Latin America is being felt most sharply by industry in Brazil, Argentina, Mexico, Venezuela, and Colombia.

Ever-growing requirements for skilled manpower, which are particularly acute in the secondary and tertiary sectors of the economy, can be satisfied through immigration of qualified workers from other, more industrially advanced, countries, particularly West and South European nations, and/or through the broadening and intensification of training programs for native workers. For the following reasons, immigration cannot be expected to fill the demand for skilled manpower to any great extent: (1) the limited availability of European workers because of their steady absorption in the expanding economy of Europe, (2) the inadequacy in several Latin American countries, and (3) the high per-capita cost of migration.

Most demographers seem to think that Latin America needs hard labor—*estancia* labor on the big estates, although some believe that in Ecuador and most other countries there is actually little need for agricultural workers. It is held that there is a superabundance of agricultural workers, especially Indians, and further that European farm workers would expect higher wages than are presently paid in Latin America. But even if there were substantial opportunities in agriculture, the fact is that the overwhelming majority of immigrants have settled in the cities, where unemployment or underemployment already is a serious problem, and where housing is seriously inadequate even without the presence of immigrants.

In his book *Immigracion y Colonizacion en la Gran Colombia,* Jesus Arango Cano asserts that immigration would improve the ethnic composition of Colombia, Venezuela, and Ecuador. While rejecting any idea of racism, he favors the "Europeanization" of the populations of these countries. But at the same time he deems it unwise to import Europeans who will "lord it" over Indian workers in Ecuador, Peru, and Bolivia.

It is the conclusion of Kingsley Davis, writing in the *Milbank Memorial Fund Quarterly* (January, 1947) that "The common belief in Latin America that the hinterlands can be settled by the simple process of bringing over masses of European immigrants and placing them on the land is a myth that never was strictly true for this region and certainly is not true today."

There are, of course, hundreds of millions of Asians who would be willing to migrate to Latin America, but Latin American countries tend toward the rigid exclusion of Asians. The resistance to Asians springs apparently from the actions of Japanese fifth columnists in Brazil and Peru during World War II, the impression made by Indian indentured laborers brought to British and Dutch possessions in the Caribbean area between 1840 and 1917, and from the competitive advantages gained by Chinese merchants in Panama, Cuba, and other countries.

Of course it is not only Latin America that tends to exclude Asians. This is true of most of the other immigrant-receiving countries as well. There is even considerable reaction against Indian immigrants in Burma and Malaya, against Chinese in Malaya and Java, and against Japanese nearly everywhere. It is the conclusion of Gyan Chand, an Indian, that Indians really have no place to go.

If people were all that is needed to fill Latin America's "open spaces," they could be supplied from the region's phenomenal natural increase. Many Latin Americans do not seem to realize, when they recommend immigration, that the population of the area is growing faster than that of any other major region of the world today. By 1986, its population will be twice as large as that of 1947. Already, the Caribbean area shows signs of overpopulation, and Mexico is constantly exerting migratory pressure on the United States border. Thus, Latin America is already in part an area of emigration. Under certain conditions it might become much more so.

Therefore, the current Latin American demand for heavy overseas immigration seems to be based largely on illusion. And as Europe becomes more urbanized and demographically stationary, it will no longer have large reserves of agricultural workers to send to Latin America. Masses of unskilled immigrants may remain, but these are precisely the groups that the Latin American economies cannot sustain. The fundamental problem in Latin America is not lack of people but lack of skills and capital.

Confronted with a population growth so rapid as to constitute a potential, if not an actual, obstacle to economic advancement, the Latin American countries as a whole have no need of the type of mass immigration that peopled the Americas in the nineteenth century. They need, at best, a selective immigration, which would contribute to economic growth without materially affecting the population. This, indeed, is exactly the kind of restrained immigration that is now occurring.

Because of historical and geographic factors, migration to Latin America differs from that to North America. The "open spaces" consist of great sections of close jungle, high mountains sealing off entire sections, and dramatic extremes of climate. Immigrants prefer the coastal cities. Richard Robbins, writing in 1958, asks:

"Why do so many Latin Americans still have their vision fixed on attracting farmers and farm laborers to colonize low-density 'open spaces' when local populations could extend the frontier from within? Is it not illusory for Latin Americans to envision a modern resumption of mass immigration when all the indices—restricted industrial opportunities, limited appeal of open land areas, restrictionist clauses in immigration laws, settlement by the simpler method of internal migration—appear to point in the opposite direction?"

The bulk of the potentially rich regions of Latin America cannot be developed dramatically because of a lack of basic capital to build roads and railroads and extend river traffic. In these areas, governmental initiative is not nearly sufficient to sustain colonization, twentieth-century style. Most important, no one can say where the immigrants would come from. Today's immigrants are city-orientated; they do not find the prospect of farm labor in the fringe areas of Latin America compelling. As for skilled European farm proprietors, emigration to the Commonwealth is favored. Paraguay is a classic example. Its 1.5 million inhabitants are thinly spread; it has rich and fertile valleys. Yet this "unrealized Garden of Eden" (as Hubert Herring puts it) is wracked by extreme poverty and by chaotic dictatorial government only recently liberated from the burden of border wars. Is it any wonder that the government must exert itself to prevent too many people from *emigrating?*

Immigration Patterns

The chief immigrant-receiving countries are Venezuela, Brazil, and Argentina, in that order. Since 1952, immigration to Latin America has been on the decline. Between 1956 and 1958, Venezuela averaged 60,000 immigrants each year, almost all from Spain, Italy, and Portugal. In the same period, Brazil averaged 48,000 immigrants, and Argentina 22,000, in both cases almost all from Spain, Italy, and Portugal. But these are gross-immigration figures. In Venezuela, only one out of three immigrants remains permanently; whereas 65,000 immigrants entered Venezuela in 1956, nearly 47,000 left. Venezuela's more than 100,000 immigrants were supposed to help augment agricultural production, but they have tended to drift from land projects into the cities. In Brazil, according to Father R. P. Fernando de Avila, S.J., internal migration from the country to the cities and from north to south will supersede European immigration. This, he says, means that mass European immigration no longer has a chance. But it does open up entirely new possibilities for qualified European labor in industry, commerce, and especially agricultural colonization. Actually, although Brazil claims that it encourages immigration, the country has not admitted a higher proportion of immigrants than the United States. Australia, proportionately, takes in seventeen times as many immigrants as Brazil, and Argentina six times as many. Ladame believes that Brazil could absorb between 100,000 and 150,000 immigrants annually, although he admits that most observers are less optimistic than he.

According to Richard Robbins, "We may expect an increased though certainly not a mass immigration to Latin America in the next five years. It will affect only slightly the over-all population growth; rather, it will expand the ranks of selected occupational groups in the population. Skilled workers and specific nationality groups will prevail: primarily Spanish and Italian workers to Argentina, Portuguese and Italians to Brazil, and Italians to Venezuela and Colombia. Bilateral agreements to attract farm settlers will continue on a small scale—the Netherlands-Brazil arrangement, operative since 1950, is typical; it has resulted in about 500 admissions annually. In addition, Latin America can probably provide asylum for some 25,000 refugees per year."

Emigration already plays a role in some Latin American countries: Puerto Rico, the West Indies, and Mexico. All Latin American republics have a quota-free status under U.S. immigration laws, but the U.S. labor demand can easily be met by Mexico alone. Until 1962 West Indian Negroes could migrate freely to Britain, just as Puerto Ricans can migrate freely to the U.S. In addition, Cubans have been pouring into the United States since the Castro revolution, but this is primarily a political rather than an economic migration. The January–February, 1958, issue of *Migration Facts and Figures,* published by the International Catholic Migration Commission in Geneva, says of immigration into Latin America:

"Although there is no doubt about the fact that there is empty space without people in Latin America, it would be misleading to conclude from this that countries naturally suited for immigration are to be discovered there. Without doubt the great period of mass immigration to South America is definitely over. This is because the combination of circumstances which brought about large-scale immigration in the last century no longer exists. ["]

It becomes evident that the Latin American countries can be regarded as effective areas for immigration only after the systematic introduction of machinery, international capital, and carefully measured immigration of a stimulating and vitalizing human element—experts, technicians, and specialized workers.

III / AFRICAN MIGRATION

Patterns of migration in Africa are amazingly complex, and lead far back in time—perhaps to the origin of man himself, for L. S. B. Leakey has found in Tanzania evidences of human activity some 1,750,000 years ago. Madagascar has experienced invasions from Indonesia, East Africa has received peoples from India and Arabia and even China, North Africa has absorbed immigrants and conquerors from the Middle East and from Southern Europe. The outbound movement from this huge continent has been largely the forced migration of the slave trade, conducted by the Arabs from East Africa and by European traders from West Africa to Europe and the Americas.

Within Africa itself populations have surged forth and back for millenniums, not by caravan or stagecoach, not by ship or airplane, but walking . . . walking . . . walking, through desert and tropical forest, mountains and plains. Movements have been influenced by the dessication of the Sahara and by lesser calamities of nature, by disease and war and economic pressures. Modern research in history, geography, linguistics, and other disciplines is probing the mysteries of these shifts of peoples and cultures, including the newer forms of labor migration and urbanization.

16 / EXPANSION OF THE BANTU

The complexities of the distribution of peoples and languages in Africa have fascinated scholars from many disciplines and have produced almost as many hypotheses as there are investigators. The impressive expansion of the Bantu-speaking peoples, beginning in distant times and continuing into the modern epoch, is one of the most challenging problems in migration studies. Professor Roland Oliver of London, editor of the Journal of African History, *has recently produced a synthesis of the latest research.*

Professor Oliver's thesis is that the expansion of the Bantu was due more to population explosion than to conquest, although conquest accompanied population growth. He likens the process, however, to the European settlement of Australia and America rather than to the Teutonic invasion in Europe in the Middle Ages. The introduction of new food crops—wheat and barley—made possible the population and cultural growth of Egypt after the fifth millennium B.C. *By the third and second millenniums* B.C. *the domestication of sorghum, millet, and dry rice facilitated the spread and increase of population through the eastern and western Sudan. To the south of this region "hunting and gathering cultures, fortified by a little . . . tenuous tropical vegeculture" predominated until about the beginning of the Christian era. The humid tropical area only then received from Southeast Asia the banana, yams, and taros. G. P. Murdock emphasized the importance of these new foods to the expansion of population and linked it all with Joseph Greenberg's explanation of the spread of the Bantu languages southward from Nigeria and the Cameroons. Oliver here argues for a different emphasis, based partly on Malcolm Guthrie's classification of the Bantu languages and, more importantly, on the beginnings of the use of iron. The cradle of the Bantu population explosion, according to Guthrie, was an elliptical area in the northern Katanga region of the Congo. Oliver accepts this and continues—*

Now what is significant here is that Guthrie's elliptical area is *not* predominantly a forested area. It is predominantly a light woodland area, intersected by many rivers, with a rainfall of about 20–30 inches a year, neither very dry, therefore, nor very humid. It is a region that corresponds ecologically with the country of the Nigerian 'middle belt' and the central Cameroons and the Ubangi-Shari watershed, to the north of the equatorial forest. It is sorghum and millet country, with first-class hunting and fishing. At its centre it is unusually well endowed with minerals, especially with iron and copper. If this is indeed the centre of the Bantu world, then we should think of its

Roland Oliver, "The Problem of the Bantu Expansion," *Journal of African History*, VII (1966), 361–376. Condensed and used by permission of the author, the *Journal of African History*, and the Cambridge University Press.

founders not as forest people, but as people of the northern woodlands, who burst through the forest barrier into the southern woodlands and established there a way of life comparable to that which they had known in the north. And, if we consider what might have been the new development which enabled them to do this, then I think we should look, not in the direction of the South-East Asian food plants, but much more likely towards the coming of the Iron Age, with its attendant improvements in woodwork, boats, tools and weapons— above all weapons for hunting and fishing. There can be no certainty on this point until we have more dates; but at least those which we have so far are possible ones. . . .

One does not have to think of Greenberg's conclusions and Guthrie's conclusions as contradictory. It is a perfectly sound interpretation to thing of them as referring to successive stages in time. Stage 1 may very well have consisted, as Guthrie himself has conjectured, in a very rapid migration, following the Congo waterways of a few dozens or hundreds of what he calls 'pre-Bantu speakers' from the central Cameroons or Ubangi-Shari woodlands to the woodlands south of the Congo forest. Stage 2 would then have consisted in the consolidation and settlement of these first migrants and their gradual expansion through the southern woodland belt from coast to coast. What Guthrie's evidence does imply is that it was here, in the southern woodland belt, that they achieved their first, main population increase. It was here that they established a bridgehead comparable to the bridgehead established by the European settlers on the Atlantic coast of North America. It was here that the parent Bantu language developed its final character. It was here, if we may use the word just once and for purposes of illustration only, that the Bantu came nearest to being a *race*. Their obvious success over against any earlier hunting, gathering and tenuously vegecultural peoples whom they found in this region would be more than adequately explained by their possession of a rudimentary iron technology and a knowledge of cereal agriculture which enabled them to take over and develop with Iron Age equipment the East African varieties of sorghums and millets. . . .

Some time during the first five centuries A.D. Madagascar, and therefore doubtless also the East African coast, were colonized by sea-borne migrants from Indonesia, and this, as I have already hinted, is therefore the stage at which we need to reconsider the influence of the South-East Asian food plants, for which Murdock has made such overriding claims. Given the previous settlement of the southern light-woodland belt by some hundreds of thousands of iron-working and cultivating Bantu speakers, who were the only large-scale food producers in Africa south of the Equator, it would be wholly logical to suppose that the coming of the South-East Asian food plants would have enabled them to expand rapidly into the more humid, more perennially watered regions to the north and the south. Given the banana and the coco-nut, and incidentally the Indian outrigger canoe, the eastern Bantu could occupy in force the humid coastal belt, and we know from Arab geographers that by the tenth century at least they had done so as far north as the Juba. In other words, when we move on from stage 2 to stage 3 of the Bantu expansion, we find that the original light woodland belt has been extended to include areas of higher rainfall, in which we know that the South-East Asian food plants, and especially the banana, have played a vital role. Where rainfall is distributed throughout the year, the banana can become not merely a seasonal luxury but a staple food. It can support a relatively dense population and requires practically no labour. The lake region provides the ideal conditions for its culture, and it would be entirely logical to suppose that a population explosion in the lake region occurred as a result of its introduction. Stage 3, I would tentatively suggest, was enacted mainly during the second half of the first millennium A.D.

Stage 4, which I believe belongs mainly to our present millennium, would then have consisted of the colonization of the remainder of the present Bantu Africa by the surplus populations generated within the area occupied at Stage 3. . . . In geographical terms what we are thinking of here is a much more gradual colonization, by the agricultural Bantu peoples of the intermediate zone of the woodlands and the forest margins, of the areas less favourable to agriculture— on the one hand the *drier* regions, the dry middle of East Africa, the dry middle of Central and South Africa, the dry middle of Angola and South-West Africa; and on the other hand the *very humid* region of the equatorial forest, through which the original Bantu ancestors must have penetrated, but which was certainly not the focal point of their expansion.

It is noteworthy that these very dry and very humid areas are precisely the areas of Bantu Africa which still contain remnant populations. In the rain forest are the Pygmies, now linguistically absorbed, but physically identifiable. In Angola and South-West Africa, as also in Central and South Africa, there are the remnants of Bushmen and Hottentots. In the dry centre of East Africa there are a whole miscellany of remnant peoples. . . .

Thus the recent picture which we see nearly everywhere in eastern and southern Africa is that of the penetration of the more marginally cultivable areas by the surplus populations generated in the more favourable, more humid areas, and in every case it is the cultivating

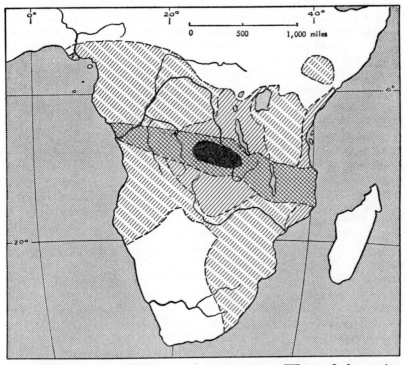

Fig.1. ▓▓ Bantu nucleus; ▨▨ stage 2 of Bantu expansion; ▨▨ stage 3 of expansion; ▨▨ stage 4 of expansion; ☐ non-Bantu.

Bantu who move in and absorb the representatives of older and less successful cultures. It is no wonder that the Bantu, especially on the eastern side of Africa, exhibit such a wide variety of physical types and social customs. Without doubt, these are attributable to the variety of earlier peoples they have absorbed.

These, then, are the four stages of the Bantu dispersion, so far as we can reconstruct them from the linguistic, cultural and traditional evidence available in 1966.

From archaeological evidence, from Portuguese documents and, increasingly, from the Shona traditions now at last being collected by Mr. Donald Abraham of the University College, Salisbury, we are beginning to have a fairly convincing outline picture of Iron Age society to the south of the Bantu nucleus, from its first humble stages around the beginning of the Christian era to a stage at which hundreds of thousands of people were grouped under powerful chiefs with large courts and elaborate rituals, supporting themselves by agriculture and stock-raising, conducting large-scale mining operations, and exporting considerable quantities of gold and ivory to the Indian Ocean markets against imports of Indian cloth and beads, and even of Chinese porcelain for the royal tables. Only two fundamental questions about this process remain unanswered. The first is whether Iron Age development can be equated with *Bantu* development. The second question, which is very close to the first, is how far this development, especially on the political side, was affected by later waves of conquest and migration from the north.

Regarding the first of these problems, there certainly seems to be some evidence that the expanding wave of Iron Age material culture rolled southwards somewhat in advance of the expanding wave of negroid physical features. . . . Nevertheless, the Kalomo culture of southern Zambia, which was in all essentials the same as the Iron Age 'A' cultures of Rhodesia, was certainly practised from the first by negroid people, and the Iron Age 'A' remained the basic material culture of the Rhodesian plateau until the Zulu invasions of the nineteenth century. The Iron Age 'B' cultures of Rhodesia are associated strictly with the stone-built capital sites, e.g., Zimbabwe. They are the specialized products of a 'court culture.' They could be identified with an immigrant aristocracy, but hardly, as some have suggested, with the first speakers of the Shona language. Therefore, I think the logical deduction is that the Iron Age 'A' culture was in origin a Bantu culture, but that it spread, as I have suggested, rather faster than the expansion of the Bantu people themselves, especially in the pastoral areas of the central plateau, where Hottentot people seem to have been quite capable of assimilating it. The second question is a more complex one, which will be more easily answered as more traditional evidence is added to that of archaeology. Almost certainly, however, we should think of the southward expansion of the Bantu as a cumulative process, in which the surplus population generated in the favourable conditions at the heart of the Bantu world was constantly pushed out toward the perimeter of an unending sequence of migration, conquest and absorption. On present evidence the explosive nucleus at the heart of the whole system would seem to have been, again and again, the Luba-speaking peoples of the Katanga.

17 / AFRICAN NEGROES TO THE AMERICAS

Stanley Elkins is an historian and social scientist of talent who, in his book Slavery, *brings not only an up-to-date outlook, but also fresh insight into the socio-psychological aspects of the forced migration of Negroes to the New World. Problems of acculturation for the Negro in the New World were fundamentally different in North America and in South America, as he vividly describes them. The yet greater differences between the Negro and the European—or even the Asian—immigrant are legible only between the lines but are well worth contemplation.*

No true picture, cursory or extended, of African culture seems to throw any light at all on the origins of what would emerge, in American plantation society, as the stereotyped "Sambo" personality. The typical West African tribesman was a distinctly warlike individual; he had a profound sense of family and family authority; he took hard work for granted; and he was accustomed to live by a highly formalized set of rules which he himself often helped to administer. If he belonged to the upper classes of tribal society—as did many who later fell victim to the slave trade—he might have had considerable experience as a political or military leader. He was the product, in any case, of cultural traditions essentially heroic in nature.

Something very profound, therefore, would have had to intervene in order to obliterate all this and to produce, on the American plantation, a society of helpless dependents.

• • •

We may suppose that every African who became a slave underwent an experience whose crude psychic impact must have been staggering and whose consequences superseded anything that had ever previously

Reprinted from *Slavery—A Problem in American Institutional and Intellectual Life* (Chicago: University of Chicago Press, 1959), pp. 97–103, 134–39, by Stanley Elkins, by permission of The University of Chicago Press. Copyright © 1959 by The University of Chicago.

happened to him. Some effort should therefore be made to picture the series of shocks which must have accompanied the principal events of that enslavement.

The majority of slaves appear to have been taken in native wars, which meant that no one—neither persons of high rank nor warriors of prowess—was guaranteed against capture and enslavement. Great numbers were caught in surprise attacks upon their villages, and since the tribes acting as middlemen for the trade had come to depend on regular supplies of captives in order to maintain that function, the distinction between wars and raiding expeditions tended to be very dim. The first shock, in an experience destined to endure many months and to leave its survivors irrevocably changed, was thus the shock of capture. It is an effort to remember that while enslavement occurred in Africa every day, to the individual it occurred just once.

The second shock—the long march to the sea—drew out the nightmare for many weeks. Under the glaring sun, through the steaming jungle, they were driven along like beasts tied together by their necks; day after day, eight or more hours at a time, they would stagger barefoot over thorny underbrush, dried reeds, and stones. Hardship, thirst, brutalities, and near starvation penetrated the experience of each exhausted man and woman who reached the coast. One traveler tells of seeing hundreds of bleaching skeletons strewn along one of the slave caravan routes. But then the man who must interest us is the man who survived—he who underwent the entire experience, of which this was only the beginning.

The next shock, aside from the fresh physical torments which accompanied it, was the sale to the European slavers. After being crowded into pens near the trading stations and kept there overnight, sometimes for days, the slaves were brought out for examination. Those rejected would be abandoned to starvation; the remaining ones—those who had been bought—were branded, given numbers inscribed on leaden tags, and herded on shipboard.

The episode that followed—almost too protracted and stupefying to be called a mere "shock"—was the dread Middle Passage, brutalizing to any man, black or white, ever to be involved with it. The holds, packed with squirming and suffocating humanity, became stinking infernos of filth and pestilence. Stories of disease, death, and cruelty on the terrible two-month voyage abound in the testimony which did much toward ending the British slave trade forever.

The final shock in the process of enslavement came with the Negro's introduction to the West Indies. Bryan Edwards, describing the arrival of a slave ship, writes of how in times of labor scarcity crowds of people would come scrambling aboard, manhandling the slaves and throwing them into panic. The Jamaica legislature eventually "corrected the enormity" by enacting that the sales be held on shore. Edwards felt a certain mortification at seeing the Negroes exposed naked in public, similar to that felt by the trader Degrandpré at seeing them examined back at the African factories. Yet here they did not seem to care. "They display . . . very few signs of lamentation for their past or of apprehension for their future condition; but . . . commonly express great eagerness to be sold." The "seasoning" process which followed completed the series of steps whereby the African Negro became a slave.

The mortality had been very high. One-third of the numbers first taken, out of a total of perhaps fifteen million, had died on the march and at the trading stations; another third died during the Middle Passage and the seasoning. Since a majority of the African-born slaves who came to the North American plantations did not come directly but were imported through the British West Indies, one may assume that the typical slave underwent an experience something like that just outlined. This was the man—one in three—who had come through it all and lived and was about to enter our "closed system." What would he be like if he survived and adjusted to that?

Actually, a great deal had happened to him already. Much of his past had been annihilated; nearly every prior connection had been severed. Not that he had really "forgotten" all these things—his family and kinship arrangements, his language, the tribal religion, the taboos, the name he had once borne, and so on—but none of it any longer carried much meaning. The old values, the sanctions, the standards, already unreal, could no longer furnish him guides for conduct, for adjusting to the expectations of a complete new life. Where then was he to look for new standards, new cues—who would furnish them now? He could now look to none but his master, the one man to whom the system had committed his entire being: the man upon whose will depended his food, his shelter, his sexual connections, whatever moral instruction he might be offered, whatever "success" was possible within the system, his very security—in short, everything.

• • •

The thoroughness with which African Negroes coming to America were detached from prior cultural sanctions should thus be partly explainable by the very shock sequence inherent in the technique of procurement. But it took something more than this to produce

"Sambo," and it is possible to overrate—or at least to overgeneralize—this shock sequence in the effort to explain what followed. A comparable experience was also undergone by slaves coming into Latin America, where very little that resembled our "Sambo" tradition would ever develop. We should also remember that, in either case, it was only the first generation that actually experienced these shocks. It could even be argued that the shock sequence is not an absolute necessity for explaining "Sambo" at all.

So whereas the Middle Passage and all that went with it must have been psychologically numbing, and should probably be regarded as a long thrust, at least, toward the end product, it has little meaning considered apart from what came later. It may be assumed that the process of detachment was completed—and, as it were, guaranteed—by the kind of "closed" authority-system into which the slave was introduced and to which he would have to adjust. At any rate, a test of this detachment and its thoroughness is virtually ready-made. Everyone who has looked into the problem of African cultural features surviving among New World Negroes agrees that the contrast between North America and Latin America is immense. In Brazil, survivals from African religion are not only to be encountered everywhere, but such carry-overs are so distinct that they may even be identified with particular tribal groups. "The Negro religions and cults," Arthur Ramos adds, "were not the only form of cultural expression which survived in Brazil. The number of folklore survivals is extremely large, the prolongation of social institutions, habits, practices and events from Africa." Fernando Ortiz, writing of Cuba in 1905, saw the African witchcraft cults flourishing on the island as a formidable social problem. One of our own anthropologists, on the other hand, despite much dedicated field work, has been put to great effort to prove that in North American Negro society any African cultural vestiges have survived at all.

Why should it be, turning once more to Latin America, that there one finds no Sambo, no social tradition, that is, in which slaves were defined by virtually complete consensus as children incapable of being trusted with the full privileges of freedom and adulthood? There, the system surely had its brutalities. The slaves arriving there from Africa had also undergone the capture, the sale, the Middle Passage. They too had been uprooted from a prior culture, from a life very different from the one in which they now found themselves. There, however, the system was not closed.

Here again the [twentieth century] concentration camp, paradoxically enough, can be instructive. There were in the camps a very small minority of the survivors who had undergone an experience different in crucial ways from that of the others, an experience which protected them from the full impact of the closed system. These people, mainly by virtue of wretched little jobs in the camp administration which offered them a minute measure of privilege, were able to carry on "underground" activities. In a practical sense the actual operations of such "undergrounds" as were possible may seem to us unheroic and limited: stealing blankets; "organizing" a few bandages, a little medicine, from the camp hospital; black market arrangements with a guard for a bit of extra food and protection for oneself and one's comrades; the circulation of news; and other such apparently trifling activities. But for the psychological balance of those involved, such activities were vital; they made possible a fundamentally different adjustment to the camp. To a prisoner so engaged, there were others who mattered, who gave real point to his existence—the SS was no longer the *only* one. Conversely, the role of the child was not the only one he played. He could take initiative; he could give as well as receive protection; he did things which had meaning in adult terms. He had, in short, alternative roles; this was a fact which made such a prisoner's transition from his old life to that of the camp less agonizing and destructive; those very prisoners, moreover, appear to have been the ones who could, upon liberation, resume normal lives most easily. It is, in fact, these people—not those of the ranks—who have described the camps to us.

It was just such a difference—indeed, a much greater one—that separated the typical slave in Latin America from the typical slave in the United States. Though he too had experienced the Middle Passage, he was entering a society where alternatives were significantly more diverse than those awaiting his kinsman in North America. Concerned in some sense with his status were distinct and at certain points competing institutions. This involved multiple and often competing "significant others." His master was, of course, clearly the chief one—but not the only one. There could, in fact, be a considerable number: the friar who boarded his ship to examine his conscience, the confessor; the priest who made the rounds and who might report irregularities in treatment to the *procurador;* the zealous Jesuit quick to resent a master's intrusion upon such sacred matters as marriage and worship (a resentment of no small consequence to the master); the local magistrate, with his eye on the king's official protector of slaves, who would find himself in trouble were the laws too widely evaded; the king's informer who received one third of the fines. For the slave the result was a certain latitude; the lines did not all converge on one man; the slave's personality, accordingly, did not have to focus on a single role. He was, true enough, primarily a slave. Yet he might in fact perform multiple roles. He could be a husband and a father (for the American slave these roles had virtually no meaning); open to him also were such activities as artisan, peddler, petty merchant, truck gardener (the law reserved to him the necessary time and a share of the proceeds, but such arrangements were against the law for Sambo); he could be a communicant in the church, a member of a religious fraternity (roles guaranteed by the most powerful institution in Latin America—comparable privileges in the American South depended on a master's pleasure). These roles were all legitimized and protected *outside* the plantation; they offered a diversity of channels for the development of personality. Not only did the individual have multiple roles open to him as a slave, but the very nature of these roles made possible a certain range of aspirations should he some day become free. He could have a fantasy-life not limited to catfish and watermelons; it was within his conception to become a priest, an independent farmer, a successful merchant, a military officer. The slave could actually—to an extent quite unthinkable in the United States —conceive of himself *as a rebel*. Bloody slave revolts, actual wars, took place in Latin America; nothing on this order occurred in the United States. But even without a rebellion, society here had a network of customary arrangements, rooted in antiquity, which made possible at many points a smooth transition of status from slave to free and which provided much social space for the exfoliation of individual character.

To the typical slave on the ante-bellum plantation in the United States, society of course offered no such alternatives. But that is hardly to say that something of an "underground"—something rather more, indeed, than an underground—could not exist in Southern slave society. And there were those in it who hardly fitted the picture of "Sambo."

The American slave system, compared with that of Latin America, was closed and circumscribed, but, like all social systems, its arrangements were less perfect in practice than they appeared to be in theory. It was possible for significant numbers of slaves, in varying degrees, to escape the full impact of the system and its coercions upon personality. The house servant, the urban mechanic, the slave who arranged his own employment and paid his master a stipulated sum each week, were all figuratively members of the "underground." Even among those working on large plantations, the skilled craftsman or the responsible slave foreman had a measure of independence not shared by his simpler brethren. Even the single slave family owned by a small farmer had a status much closer to that of house servants than to that of a plantation labor gang. For all such people there was a margin of space denied to the majority; the system's authority-structure claimed their bodies but not quite their souls.

Out of such groups an individual as complex and as highly developed as William Johnson, the Natchez barber, might emerge. Johnson's diary reveals a personality that one recognizes instantly as a type—but a type whose values came from a sector of society very different from that which formed Sambo. Johnson is the young man on the make, the ambitious free-enterpriser of American legend. He began life as a slave, was manumitted at the age of eleven, and rose from a poor apprentice barber to become one of the wealthiest and most influential Negroes in ante-bellum Mississippi. He was respected by white and black alike, and counted among his friends some of the leading public men of the state.

It is of great interest to note that although the danger of slave revolts (like Communist conspiracies in our own day) was much overrated by touchy Southerners; the revolts that actually did occur were in no instance planned by plantation laborers but rather by Negroes whose qualities of leadership were developed well outside the full coercions of the plantation authority-system. Gabriel, who led the revolt of 1800, was a blacksmith who lived a few miles outside Richmond; Denmark Vesey, leading spirit of the 1822 plot at Charleston, was a freed Negro artisan who had been born in Africa and served several years aboard a slave-trading vessel; and Nat Turner, the Virginia slave who fomented the massacre of 1831, was a literate preacher of recognized intelligence. Of the plots that have been convincingly substantiated (whether they came to anything or not), the majority originated in urban centers.

For a time during Reconstruction, a Negro elite of sorts did emerge in the South. Many of its members were Northern Negroes, but the Southern ex-slaves who also comprised it seem in general to have emerged from the categories just indicated. Vernon Wharton, writing of Mississippi, says:

A large portion of the minor Negro leaders were preachers, lawyers, or teachers from the free states or from Canada. Their education and their independent attitude gained for them immediate favor and leadership.

Of the natives who became their rivals, the majority had been urban slaves, blacksmiths, carpenters, clerks, or waiters in hotels and boarding houses; a few of them had been favored body-servants of affluent whites.

The William Johnsons and Denmark Veseys have been accorded, though belatedly, their due honor. They are, indeed, all too easily identified, thanks to the system that enabled them as individuals to be so conspicuous and so exceptional and, as members of a group, so few.

18 / THE *OIBU-DUDU* (WHITE-BLACK) IMMIGRANTS TO LAGOS, NIGERIA

The African was profoundly affected by his contact with European-American civilization—an impact on attitudes and values and personality. Even when he was a slave and the contact was perhaps but brief, he became a changed man. He tended to overvalue the strange new culture and he could not absorb all of it at once. His reaction was illustrated at least superficially by the fact that captives and others who were taken to Sierra Leone built villages above Freetown that they called by names such as Regent and Gloucester and also by the fact that the returnees from America who created Liberia not only dressed like Americans, but fashioned their constitution and their flag after the United States models and now actually use American currency and coinage. The "Americo-Liberians" became an upper class that often was as much resented by the indigenous population as if they had been white overlords.

A fascinating example of the still further extension of this socio-psychological phenomenon is the story of the migration to Lagos of Africans back from Sierra Leone and Brazil. Their contact with Europeans often had been meager, and they often were closely related to the other Africans already settled in the Nigerian city, but they nevertheless were set apart. The ensuing vignette of the impact of culture change induced by the combination first of emigration and then of immigration is by Professor Spencer H. Brown of Western Illinois University, who has written a social history of Lagos (still unpublished).

Spencer H. Brown, "The *Oibo-Dudu* (White-Black) Immigrants to Lagos, Nigeria," a paper written especially for this volume.

One of the most humanly interesting aspects of migration as a factor in cultural diffusion is the manner in which migrants are received when they return to their native society. The reception of the primarily Yoruba Africans from Freetown, Sierra Leone, where they had been landed by British naval cruisers after being liberated from slaving vessels by their Yoruba kinsmen in and around Lagos, provides an excellent example of the cultural alienation that even forced migration often produces for returnees.

The distinctive terminology used to designate such returnees was indicative of the separate status they occupied. No longer were they accepted members of the "people of Lagos"; rather they were Sierra Leoneans or Saros. As such, they were looked upon as foreigners who were potentially more dangerous to the political, economic, and social *status quo* of the native Lagosians than were the Europeans. Even more striking evidence of the distinct position occupied by the Sierra Leoneans can be found in the repeated native references to them throughout the 1850's and early 1860's as *oibo dudu,* or white-black men. In some instances, Sierra Leoneans such as James White, a catechist for the Church Missionary Society, and Samuel Crowther, Jr., son of Bishop Crowther and a secular employee of the C.M.S., were simply referred to as Englishmen or *oibo,* a term used of all whites.

The implications of such terminology seem obvious. For the native Lagosian viewing the returned Yoruba from Freetown, the similarity of skin coloration was of lesser importance than the divergencies in attitudes, language, dress, and customs. To varying degrees, depending upon his wealth, the amount of his formal education, and the length and nature of his contact with Europeans, the Sierra Leonean emulated the European when he returned to Lagos. The adoption of European ways was usually greeted with derision by the Europeans themselves, who persisted in irrationally equating skin coloration with cultural uniformity. But for the first few decades most native Lagosians were willing to accept the Sierra Leoneans as what they purported to be—*oibo* or *oibo-dudu.*

Benjamin Campbell, British consul at Lagos from mid-1853, in a dispatch to the Foreign Office in April, 1857, probably summed up the Lagosian attitude toward the Sierra Leoneans as accurately as any European could.

For some time past there has existed a deep feeling of jealousy on the part of the Native inhabitants of Lagos towards the Sierra Leone emigrants, created, no doubt, by their superior intelligence and the higher social position obtained by them over the Natives, who do not hesitate openly to express their aversion to men, who they state were sold from this place only a few years since, and who have now returned so much their superiors, occupying a considerable portion of the best part of the town and enjoying so large a portion of its trade.

The Yoruba who remained in Sierra Leone and who from time to time sent gifts and money to his relatives in the Lagos area was generally admired and respected. The Yoruba who returned to Lagos, however, whose assumption of European ways was visibly apparent and whose role as an intermediary between the native Lagosians and the Europeans frequently gave him a position of economic dominance, was viewed in an entirely different light. It is not without significance that the two attempts to expel the British during the 1850's, both organized by Madame Tinubu, a member of the royal family and a prominent trader, were also directed at the expulsion of the Sierra Leoneans.

Though the adoption of European ways by the Sierra Leoneans was far from complete and universal, the impact upon Lagos society of some 2,500 Saros who arrived during the 1850's, only a small portion of whom were thoroughly Europeanized, is a dramatic indication of the cultural consequences of migration upon the individual and his native society.

19 / MIGRATIONS TO THE PARE MOUNTAINS

Dr. Isaria Kimambo, author of a history of the Pare people, is lecturer in history in the University of East Africa, Dar es Salaam. He has carefully used the techniques of oral history. In this specially written chapter, he relates and analyzes the peopling of the Pare Mountains —a process that is historically unique, but that is significant, nevertheless, for the interpretation of other African migrations as well as of migration in general and the resultant blending of cultures.

Students of human migrations have often taken interest in the various reasons for human movements. People like the Gypsies have often made scholars wonder whether there is an unexplainable drive for

Isaria Kimambo, "Migrations to The Pare Mountains," prepared for this volume.

human beings to migrate. However, cannot human migrations in most cases be explained by the peculiar circumstances connected with human needs? This discussion aims to illustrate this hypothesis by examining migrations over a period of about 500 years before 1900 to a small area in Africa. Attention will be focused upon the reasons for the migrations and their results in this particular area.

The Pare country is situated on a range of mountains known by the same name and found between the Usambara Mountains and Kilimanjaro, in northeastern Tanzania. The neighbors of the Pare in the north are the Chagga of Kilimanjaro. In the east are the Taita, in the south the Sambaa, and in the west the Masai. The ranges of mountains (including Usambara) run from near the coast up to Mount Kilimanjaro. In the east the mountains gradually pass into the Taita Hills and finally into the dry flat country often called the Nyika Plains. On the west the mountains slope steeply into the Pangani Valley, across which is the Masai Steppe. In the southwest, across the Pangani Valley are the Nguu (or Nguru) Mountains. The dominant migrations naturally have followed routes from the plains to the mountains, for reasons which will become obvious.

We can identify four main factors causing migrations to the Pare Mountains. The first cause was connected with natural calamities—droughts and famines. We know that such calamities frequently affected the Nyika Plains in the historical period, that is, since the second quarter of the nineteenth century. It is reasonable to assume, therefore, that such crisis periods had played a part in the history of population movements in this region for many years. At least Pare traditions indicate that the earliest remembered migrations to the region took place far back in the legendary past, probably as early as the beginning of the present millennium. These migrations may have come from an area of population pressure in the Taita Hills near Mount Kilimanjaro. But in the legends we can detect idioms of famines, for most of the groups say that stealing food was the beginning of the trouble that finally caused their movement.

Thirteen to ten generations ago (or about sixteenth and seventeenth centuries) several groups of people arrived on the Pare Mountains from the Taita Hills. These migrations may be connected with the movement of the coastal group of the northeastern Bantu speaking peoples. Their migrations often are mentioned as being connected with the mythical center known as Shungwaya, but the spread of these movements to the Pare Mountains indicates that they represented wider migrations from the Nyika Plains rather than a migration from a single center. Unlike the earlier migrations which followed a northern route near Lake Jipe, these later migrations followed a southern route leading to the southern division of the Pare Mountains. In this period, too, there were migrations from the southern side of the country, that is, from the Nguu Mountains. Luckily this second period of migrations to the Pare Mountains is nearer to us in time, and Pare traditions can give more evidence about the causes behind them. We know that about ten generations ago there was a famine that affected a large area of East Africa. It is remembered on the Pare Mountains as *Mbofu* or *Safu* and on the Nguu Mountains as *Kidyakingo*. This famine and similar calamities may have caused the movements of the various groups that arrived in the Pare country during this period. The groups themselves indicated their concern about these natural calamities by emphasizing irrigation channels and by assigning to these irrigation channels an important ritual position in their lives. They also gave a special position to those who claimed to possess the power of making rain and of bringing prosperity to the country. This was a period when rain-making political leadership became prominent in South Pare.

We may assume that in periods of drought and famine people moved from the plains and hills to the more favorable highlands. The Pare Mountains were in an intermediate position. They were better in terms of rain and water supplies than the Taita Hills and the Nyika Plains. But in times of prolonged drought they were more vulnerable than either Usambara or Kilimanjaro. This situation was illustrated during the famine known on the Pare Mountains as *Mnyime* (1888–92), when a number of Pare groups moved to greener areas in both Kilimanjaro and Usambara.

Thus movements caused by droughts and famines may be said to be a response of people to their environment. For agricultural people this had to be movement in search of more productive agricultural areas. It was therefore natural that people should move to highland areas where agricultural life was more practicable. They emphasized rituals and other methods that would prevent further occurrence of drought and famine. Irrigation channels and rain-making symbolized the practical and the ritual or religious response to environmental factors.

The second cause of migration to the Pare Mountains was war. The earliest remembered migrations to South Pare (about sixteen generations ago, or about the end of the fifteenth century) were caused by a civil war in Ugweno. According to Ugweno traditions the war was a crisis coming from the internal frictions of an expanding society. But the movement of the Wabwambo from Ugweno to South Pare was an important event since it initiated the process of peopling South Pare, a process that was to continue for centuries. Subsequent wars outside the Pare country were to send more groups of people to different sections of the Pare Mountains. In the eighteenth century the Kilindi took over political power in Usambara, and during this crisis period a number of Sambaa families sought refuge on the Pare Mountains. Before the end of the century struggles for political power began among the various Chagga chiefdoms of Kilimanjaro, and a number of their displaced people also found refuge on the Pare Mountains.

One may ask why political refugees would go to the Pare country. Were the Pare supporters of persecuted peoples? Generally speaking, the movement of displaced people into the Pare Mountains is an indication that the Pare were not isolated from their neighbors, but enjoyed constant exchange of ideas, goods, and population. Internally, however, granting asylum was an important political symbol. Among the Pare a ruler who failed to protect his people, or to treat them fairly, was faced with mass movement of people from his district to another ruler's district. A movement of a mistreated non-Pare group to a Pare district had the same meaning, that is, that a good ruler's protection was being sought.

The third factor in migrations to the Pare country was trade. Exchange of commodities between the Pare and their neighbors has been a prominent feature in the economic life of the Pare. As far as the Pare were concerned iron was the most important product. It would be interesting to know how Pare iron trade influenced Pare movements into Kilimanjaro, for example. But Sambaa trade activities on the Pare Mountains had important consequences for immigration into the Pare country. Quite early in Pare history Sambaa groups started to trade in deer or *mpaa* skins obtained through hunting in the Pare country. *Mpaa* was a special kind of deer that was found only in the Pare country, probably because its species had been exhausted in Usambara. Yet the skin of *mpaa* was required for a ritual that also was known as *mpaa*. This *mpaa* ritual, performed just before the birth of the first child, was one of a series of rituals (known as *ulezi*) observed to make the child a lawful member of the society.

It was the duty of the father to supply the *mpaa* skin. But since not all fathers could go to the Pare Mountains to hunt, some Sambaa specialized in this trade. They went to the Pare country, hunted *mpaa*, took the skins to Usambara and exchanged them for goat skins. They then returned the goat skins to the Pare country and exchanged them for goats and cattle. In this way Sambaa traders were accumulating wealth in the Pare country. Some eventually decided to give up hunting and take care of the herds they already had accumulated in the Pare region.

In the nineteenth century this Sambaa trade in the Pare country got twisted into something new. In the earlier period the Sambaa hunters obtained permission from Pare rulers to hunt on the plains. The exchange of goods was carried out on the mountains in Pare markets, and the livestock accumulated were kept in Pare districts and herded with Pare livestock. But in the second half of the nineteenth century Sambaa individuals, posing as hunters, wanted to build villages on the Pare plains. Pare rulers gave the Sambaa permission to do so because the plains were not being used by the Pare themselves, since they had preferred to live on the top of the mountains. The establishment of Sambaa villages on the Pare plains had far-reaching results on the mountains. The immediate effect was to expand slave-trading activities on the Pare Mountains. The Sambaa colonists acted as middlemen in the coastal caravan trade and encouraged Pare communities to raid one another, thus increasing the human cargo transported to the coast. This was the negative effect of the Sambaa movement into the Pare Mountains. It helped to deepen the effects of the slave trade on Pare society, as exemplified in the fragmentation of the political units that had been formed on the Pare Mountains.

Two positive contributions of Sambaa penetration into the Pare country may be cited. First, the Sambaa brought an important social change to the area. By starting villages on the plains the Sambaa demonstrated to the Pare that a reasonable living was possible on the lowlands and thus many Pare people began to move to the plains. Secondly, the Sambaa helped to spread to the interior coastal influences such as the Swahili language, rectangular houses, and belief in spirit possession.

The Sambaa could exercise such influence better than the Swahili traders themselves because the Sambaa made permanent residences in the Pare country. This spread of Swahili culture, a process that still continues, has helped to bridge the historic dichotomy between the coast and the hinterland of Tanzania.

The fourth reason for movements to the Pare Mountains was the search for tax money. This was a colonial phenomenon that was only beginning to manifest itself in 1900, but that throughout the colonial period affected a large part of Tanzania as well as other territories. Although migrant labor did not affect Tanzania as much as it did Central Africa, at least southern Tanzania witnessed considerable movement of its people to other areas in search of work. Early in the 1900's a community was formed in the north on the shores of Lake Jipe by migrant laborers from southern Tanzania. A group of people from a fishing village called Chiuru, on Lake Malawi, traveled to Tanga in order to earn money by offering their labor. They had to do this because the German government had imposed a hut tax in the country since 1898. In Tanga the migrant laborers from Lake Malawi were successful in getting jobs on some estates, but they were not happy with the new mode of living. They were used to a fishing life and therefore were eagerly seeking a place where they could us their traditional occupation and yet collect money for it. When they heard about the existence of a lake in the interior they decided to move to the region, and there they started a fishing community that supplied fish to several local markets.

In this case of migrant labor the Pare were on the receiving end. But the Pare themselves had to try to earn money too. Although the story of movements of the Pare to other areas is not covered in this migration account, it is important to remember that the search for money affected many colonial societies in Africa. In areas where a cash crop was adopted early, as in Kilimanjaro, the need to seek work outside the people's home territory was lessened. For the Pare, cash cropping did not take form as early as in Kilimanjaro, but various patterns of trade and work in towns compensated for the slow start in cash crop economy.

What the story of migrations into the Pare Mountains has demonstrated is how an intermixture of population can be blended together in forming a culture. Whether the initial movement was caused by famine, war, trade, or need to earn money for taxes, once the people arrived in the area they formed a community with its own culture. New immigrants were quickly absorbed into the older community, and the newcomers also contributed something to the growth of its culture. The formation of the fishing community on Lake Jipe is the best example. The handful of "Nyasa" immigrants who arrived on the shores of the lake realized that this was not their country. Therefore, they went to the mountains to get a Pare ritual leader to perform a ritual for them so that they could have a successful beginning in this new community. Their initial success also attracted Pare people to move to the region from the mountains. Thus what started as a community of foreigners was soon to become an intermixture of population outnumbered by Pare speakers. In the end this community became a Pare community speaking the Pare language and holding Pare values. But important changes had been brought to both the Pare and the Nyasa members of the community. The Pare had adopted fishing, and the Nyasa, like the Pare themselves, had adopted cultivation and herding.

Certainly this is the way many human societies are formed. What has been called the melting pot in American history is another example of this acculturation of immigrants to an area. Throughout history the mixing and mingling of populations have been characteristics of human societies. Thus the intermixture of populations not only affords an opportunity to reflect on a long line of human history, but also indicates how ridiculous our attempts to classify human beings into rigid categories can be.

20 / EMIGRATION AND RETURN OF THE CHAGGA

The Chagga live close to the Pare, and this selection on outbound movement and temporary migration serves as a complement to Dr. Kimambo's essay, which emphasizes an earlier period and an inward movement of people. If it seems to the reader that Mrs. Rogers is simply talking about a group of people adapting to the twentieth century, it must be recalled that the way these men of the mountain come into the twentieth century is not primarily through television but through contact with the town.

Mrs. Robert (Susan Geiger) Rogers is an American now working for the Ph.D. in history at the University of East Africa, Dar es Salaam. While living at Marangu, on the southern slope of Mt. Kilimanjaro, she conducted in person and through a corps of informants a survey of the reasons for, and the effects of, various types of migration from the Mountain.

The Chagga of Kilimanjaro are among the most mobile people of Tanzania. Although the rapid change that has taken place in their society often has been attributed to the influence of coffee and the missions, their progress also has been associated with their mobility.

Susan Geiger Rogers, "Emigration and Return of the Chagga," researched and written for this volume.

In every major town and in many rural settlements in Tanzania as well as in Kenya and Uganda, Chaggas are to be found performing a wide range of tasks and often occupying positions of high responsibility in government and business.

There is an apparent paradox here, because for the large majority of these people there is no substitute for snowcapped Kilimanjaro. There is, in fact, an almost fanatical love of the land, even among the landless, and suspicion always has been directed against anyone who has appeared to endanger the rights of the tribe to maintain its hold on the mountain. Awareness of the land problems in neighboring Kenya and on nearby Mt. Meru served to magnify Chagga fears. But the paradox of mobility and attachment is resolved by the fact that despite the ease with which they migrate, virtually all the Chaggas intend to return to the Mountain to take up land, to start a business, to retire with the money made elsewhere, or at least to die.

The problem of land shortage has been one of the major causes of the pattern of large-scale, temporary emigration. The alienation of land on the mountainside began during the German colonial period, and after World War I the British administration realienated German estates to Greek, South African, and British settlers. Rapid population growth, from about 155,000 in 1931 to 360,000 by 1964, and the need for land to grow coffee and subsistence crops, brought increasing pressure and resentment against the belt of European holdings that limited natural expansion. Below this belt lay the plains, a vast expanse of arid bush where the problems of irrigation and tsetse-fly control made settlement unattractive. Unwilling to work for settlers, who paid low wages and were associated with an attempt to destroy the infant native coffee industry during the 1920's, many Chaggas without sufficient land for self-support began to seek employment further afield.

Had other areas similar to Uchagga (Chaggaland) been available for cultivation, emigration might have been predominantly from rural to rural, but as such land was already intensely occupied the major flow of Chagga émigrés was diverted to the towns. Having its beginnings in the 1920's and reaching considerable numbers in the late 1940's and 50's, this urban migration increased and developed fairly steadily, drawing, of course, from the areas of the Mountain where land pressure was most keenly felt. With easy and rapid access both to the coast and to Nairobi via rail or road, the Chaggas were not hindered by isolation or lack of good communications and transportation.

To understand more fully the nature of this emigration, one must also see it in the context of the rapidly changing mountain society which, because of the growth of coffee as a cash crop, was drawn quickly into a modern money economy in the early 1930's. A proverb from the Machame section of the Mountain warns that "sitting buttocks never carry straw." That is, if someone wants to make something of himself, he must go out in search of the means. Traditionally, when a young Chagga decided to marry, his parents would supply him and his fiancée with a plot of land, usually undeveloped. When the plot had been at least partially developed and a house built the young man could marry. This custom of establishing a homestead persisted, but it became increasingly difficult for the parent to provide his sons with the necessary land. The result has been an exodus of young men to centers of employment where money might be earned to buy land and to pay dowry. Often, the young émigré has returned after a few years either with sufficient funds to establish himself on a plot or with the trained skill to become on the Mountain a carpenter, a mason, a tailor, or the like. Sometimes, too, a man has gone out to work on an even more temporary basis during the three or four months in the year when there is little work to be done on the land.

The second major factor that has contributed to emigration of a different nature is education—some would call it over-education. Fortunately for the Chaggas, Catholic and Lutheran competition for converts has expressed itself in the building of schools. In 1955, of the school-age children eligible for Standards I–IV, 80 per cent were in school—about twice the figure for the country as a whole. Many go on to Standard VIII, and after completion of this education a boy feels that he deserves a job—a good job. If he fails to find the job on the Mountain or nearby in Moshi town, he naturally heads for a larger town in search of work, adventure, and independence.

Furthermore, because of the large number of primary schools, a high proportion of the Chagga have been able to take advantage of secondary schools, technical training, and higher education. In the 1940's the majority of Tanganyika students at Makerere College, in Uganda, were Chagga. Under the colonial regime the Chaggas therefore held many of the positions of responsibility throughout the country that were open to Africans. After national independence in 1961, with the expansion of government and professional opportunities and the stated policy of situating top level civil servants outside their own tribal areas, the number of educated Chaggas serving away from Kilimanjaro grew even more rapidly. It is not surprising that the Chaggas, who represent only 4 per cent of Tanzania's 10,000,000 people, account for approximately 10 per cent of the Tanzanians mentioned in *Who's Who in East Africa.*

On the whole, these career émigrés, with their high level of education and broadened world outlook, share the attitude of other Chaggas with regard to an eventual return to Kilimanjaro. In his *Survey of Dar es Salaam,* J. A. K. Leslie refers to this type of Chagga emigrant when he states that the Chagga are not among the main traditional groups of migrants to that city, but are part of a newer, more modern stream "using new modes of transport, often brought here on transfer in government service or in that of firms, educated, and secure, career men coming to spend a working life in Dar es Salaam and then retire home." Away in the city they form associations because they "genuinely feel the need for 'someone of their own kind' in a mainly uneducated, Muslim and coastal town."

Apart from the factors of increased land pressure and education, the Chaggas themselves cite periods of change and trouble as the greatest stimulants to emigration in the past. In the last century tribal and civil wars were responsible for the internal movements of large numbers of people, whereas during the present century both World Wars took men away as porters and askaris and at the same time opened up new opportunities (through skills learned) to work and make money elsewhere. Contacts resulting in travel to the coast, commencing with the coming of the first Arab slave caravans that passed Kilimanjaro on their northern route to the lake area in the mid-nineteenth century, developed steadily in later years and were stimulated by the building of the Tanga-Moshi railroad, the first line to be completed by the German colonial administration in Tanganyika. A famine in the Rombo area of the Mountain during the 1930's is remembered as being responsible for a sudden rise in the number of emigrants. Furthermore, the need to find money to pay taxes also has encouraged the Chaggas to leave the Mountain in search of livelihood. And finally, personal and family quarrels seem often to have been solved by the departure of one or more of the people involved.

The great majority of Chaggas interviewed indicated that the wish to gain wealth through employment was the main motivation for Chagga emigration. The people are eager to improve their standard of living, which is probably already the highest in Tanzania. Stimulating standards have been set, not so much by European settlers or civil servants as by wealthy Chagga coffee farmers on the mountain, whose cement houses, well kept compounds, and modern conveniences nestle among the Chagga huts and banana plantations.

Mombasa, as the nearest large commercial center, has long been the most popular destination for Chagga emigrants; until the recent monetary changes Mombasa and Nairobi in Kenya have figured more importantly in the movements of Chagga workers than any Tanzanian towns. Other places that have attracted Chagga émigrés are Dar es Salaam, Tanga, Arusha, Mwanza, and several towns in Mbulu district. Although the Chagga proverb "To travel is father; to stay at home is mother" still holds true in the majority of cases, a number of informants pointed out that with increased educational opportunities for girls, women are now almost as mobile as men. The fact that more men than women leave the Mountain, however, is at least partly substantiated by the current oversupply at home of marriageable Chagga girls. This situation is cited as one of the reasons for the increase in prostitution in the town of Moshi. It must be remembered, however, that to many of the older more tradition-conscious Chagga, a girl who goes to town and lives alone without a husband, regardless of whether she is a secretary, a seamstress, or a waitress, is labeled a prostitute.

There are undoubtedly other factors involved in the preponderance of women, however, because most émigrés, although they may postpone marriage, will return to the Mountain to take wives. The reasons given for wanting to marry within the tribe hark back to custom and tradition, with particular stress upon the character and family background of one's future spouse. The Chaggas consider themselves superior and all non-Chaggas are called *vyasaka,* implying inferiority and backwardness. Marriage is one of the most common reasons given for returning home, but in many a case the ceremony will mark a temporary visit, after which the man will return to his job elsewhere. If he has saved enough money he will establish his wife in a house of their own (an absolute necessity, according to custom in some parts of the mountain). If not, she will live with his parents until he inherits or can afford to build a house. Seldom will the new wife join her husband at his place of work. In an interview with employees at Ngorongoro Crater Lodge, fifty-two out of seventy of whom are Chaggas, Mr. Stanley Kimambo stated that although the Chaggas working at the Lodge intend to remain there "till God knows," few bring their wives. The pattern of living arrangements is, of course, somewhat different among highly educated Chaggas who fill government, administrative, and professional posts and can afford to hire people to maintain their property on the mountain while their wives stay with them.

For the majority of Chaggas, this self-imposed bachelorhood and the circumstances of living in town—so different from life on the

Mountain where social life is centered around the family, the clan, and the *"mtaa"* (area chiefdom) in that order—has led to the close co-operation of émigrés in alien places. It is worth remembering that the Chaggas themselves are of different origins (mainly Kamba, Taita, Masai, Pare, and Shamba) and that the gradual amalgamation of over twenty distinct chiefdoms has occurred only in the past fifty years. Dialects of Kichagga continue to differ from area to area, and the civil wars and clan rivalries of the past are well remembered. In a very real sense, then, Chagga émigrés have aided the cause of unity on Kilimanjaro. For example, despite the long-felt hatred and distrust existing between their chiefdoms on the Mountain, men from Kibosho who are living away and without their families find much in common with men of Machame who are in a similar situation. In the unfamiliar circumstances of town life (especially for drinking and socializing) local differences are underplayed.

Since tribal associations are now discouraged by government, many of the people interviewed were reluctant to emphasize their importance to Chagga émigrés. It would appear that the aims of the Chagga Associations that flourished in the 1950's were (1) to provide members of the community with opportunities to get together for social purposes, particularly for the celebration of holidays, local or otherwise, (2) to assist members in need or in trouble, and (3) to serve as centers for gathering and disseminating news from Chaggaland. A letter from the secretary of the Mombasa Chagga Association to the Paramount Chief dated 24 November 1955 indicates this association's concern for maintaining the good name of the Chagga. The secretary states that the association does not approve of the presence in Mombasa of the increasing number of young, unemployed boys from the mountain who are drifting around and causing trouble:

> If a real Mchagga comes to Mombasa and sees these youths moving about like loafers he will feel rather embarrassed. Therefore steps must be taken by the Chagga Council to cope with this problem or we shall soon find ourselves confronted by a generation of loafers.

Similar concerns were felt by the Chagga Association in Dar es Salaam, which in 1951 established a hospital visiting committee, a housing committee, and an employment committee and hoped to cooperate with the associations in Mombasa, Tanga, Arusha, and other towns.

On their frequent visits home (as often as monthly from Mombasa) émigrés are eager to impress their friends and families with the positive aspects of their work and life. Usually, particularly if employment opportunities are good, a Chagga will write home encouraging others to come and, regardless of his personal circumstances, will provide at least temporary lodging for the new arrivals.

Most parents encourage their children to go out in search of work, but they also increasingly fear that the young people may marry *vyasaka* or never return.

Unable to give their children land in the traditional fashion, many parents now strive to give them education as their rightful inheritance. Nevertheless, there is a growing realization on Kilimanjaro that education is a double-edged sword that may cut a path to opportunity, on the one hand, but will slash deeply, on the other hand, into the traditional roots of family relationships. Although education will take one's children away for schooling and subsequently, it is hoped, for jobs, prestige may be gained by the parents whose offspring are successful in acquiring money and status in modern terms. One cannot mistake the pride in a father's voice when he tells of his sons and daughters—one an engineer in Nairobi, another a teacher in Arusha, and a third a typist in Dar es Salaam. Fully aware of the changes taking place in their society, many parents say that although they don't encourage their children to go away, "they may if they want to," or "they do anyway."

In questions asked to elicit ideas on the changes, if any, noticeable in an émigré as a result of living and working away, several informants drew the distinction between émigrés living in rural areas, who changed little, and those working in towns and cities, who changed considerably. Observations varied widely. Most Chaggas were in agreement that the émigré's manner of speech changes noticeably; he "forgets" his vernacular and is likely to speak Swahili (good Swahili if he has been to the coast) or mix languages. He may, in fact, change his speech intentionally "to attract attention to himself," using English or Swahili slang and expressions. People also agreed that the émigré dresses differently—"more smartly"—with shoes, hats, and watches being mentioned.

On questions of manners and ideas respondents differed widely in their attitudes towards émigrés. Some saw the émigré as one who exhibits "an assumed superiority," vanity, obstinacy, cunning, and corruption. One informant stated that the Chagga émigré will not co-operate with anyone except the people he has been away with and "forgets" Chagga customs. He is "avaricious" and steals. He smokes and is bad, different, and awkward. He acts like a "townie" and looks down on the villagers. More neutral in tone were observations that the Chagga émigré is much more talkative, often relating stories of exotic events and of his successes or failures. His "town ideas" include wanting his meals at convenient times and never wanting a minute to pass without something to do. He is seen as "modern," and European or foreign characteristics often are attributed to him. He is often referred to as an "Mswahili."

On the positive side, informants found returning Chaggas better informed. "They have seen many things apart from the Mountain," are clean and neat in appearance, healthy in body, sociable, and gentle. The émigré is thought to have "better manners of staying with people," or "the manners of the people with whom he lived." Some said he is more polite to elders. "Don't worry," said one old man confidently, "he knows what it is to be a Chagga!" And, with admiration, "He has a cool mind, especially about business."

One may only conclude that the experience of living and working away varies considerably from individual to individual and provokes a subsequent variety of changes in his manner and character that are noted by the people at home. Many informants stressed that you simply couldn't tell how a person was going to act until he returned and that it was necessary to wait and see how the émigré had changed before judging him.

Because of the continuous flow of men between the Mountain and the towns—particularly the coast—Kilimanjaro has been soundly buffeted with cross currents of ideas. The returnees have brought with them a broader and more open outlook, in part the result of the very practical realization that in order to get along when working and living among aliens one has to adjust, compromise, and become more flexible. In the most general terms this is expressed as "getting along with others," but more specific mention is made of new forms of hospitality such as inviting people to one's home for "talk, lunch, or to arrange a gathering." To the influence of returnees is also credited the custom of sitting together at a table or on a mat to eat, as well as the use of knives and forks and other practices involving eating. In the realm of practical innovations, returnees are recognized as having helped to improve the standard of living on the Mountain, demonstrating new and better methods of house building and masonry (particularly the replacement of the traditional round hut with a square house), new ways of doing practical work such as carpentry and sewing, better agricultural methods, and modern concepts of business and of shop keeping. The modern "bar" may well have been introduced by returning émigrés, as well as the making and drinking of various kinds of beer. Many people emphasized that returnees often are leaders in the formation of associations, co-operatives, and groups for business or agricultural purposes. The returnee reads more and is not so fanatically religious—a fact often lamented by the older, more conservative Christians on the mountain. He is likely to be more concerned about his health and the health of others, discouraging such practices as sleeping in the same room with animals.

Émigrés who have spent most of their working lives at the coast often adopt Islam and return to join the small but significant "pockets" of Muslims on the Mountain. Returnees also have introduced from the coast Swahili colloquial expressions and other practices associated with Swahili culture, such as carrying a stick when walking and wearing a "fez" (this often is also adopted by Chagga Christians who have worked in Mombasa). The use of rice and coconuts in cooking and the practice of frying foods also are considered coastal innovations. New dances and ways of dressing brought back from the towns are said to have greatly influenced the teenage population, whereas the only practice specifically brought back by and for women appears to be combing hair with a "hot comb" for the purpose of straightening it.

On the negative side, informants pointed out that returnees often disregard tribal sexual mores and have been instrumental in trying to abolish the dowry system and to introduce changes in marriage practices. Some were given to thieving and gambling, and not a few had returned as witch doctors.

In assessing the responses of informants to the above questions, it is important to keep in mind that in Chaggaland temporary emigration is an accepted fact with most people. It has occurred at all levels of society and has attracted, for various reasons, people from the entire range of the population, from the educated career workers to the poorly educated or uneducated landless who see emigration solely as a chance to make some money. Attitudes toward those who go away, therefore, vary to a great extent. Some Chaggas stated in a matter-of-fact way that they had no feelings at all toward émigrés and really couldn't see why anyone should want to ask. Others said that they felt "inferior" or "envious" in the shadow of successful émigrés and suggested that those who left the Mountain had special attributes such as "push," "self-reliance," and "a different ability of talking." "But wherever they go," said a farmer, "they depend on us here on the Mountain to produce the food they eat!"

There can be little doubt that the pattern of temporary emigration established by the Chaggas has had an important psychological impact upon the inhabitants of Chaggaland, forcing, as it has, the examination of old ideas, attitudes, and values. In assessing the success of the Chaggas as a tribe and their position among the most advanced people of Tanzania, one must consider their high degree of mobility as a significant determining factor.

21 / THE GREAT TREK

In South Africa two powerful migratory movements clashed in epic style. One was the southward-reaching thrust of the Bantu tribesmen, especially the Zulus. The other was the European settlement by the Dutch, beginning at the Cape of Good Hope in 1652 and developing gradually into the Boers' push inland. Here was a phenomenon quite different from that along the west coast of Africa, where Europeans of many nationalities built trading posts and forts on the coast but made little attempt (until the nineteenth century) to establish rule over natives or land in the interior. It contrasted also with the situation in North America where European agriculturalists confronted Indian hunters, scattered and sparse. In South Africa Boer cattle-breeders, as they trekked inland from the Cape, soon faced up against a solid wall of Bantu cattle-breeders. There was no room for compromise, and the meeting was bloody, the whole situation aggravated by the antagonism between the Boers and the British who took control of the Cape in the early nineteenth century. From the first one of the chief causes of conflict was the more tolerant policy of the English toward the natives and the abolition of slavery. In 1820 some 5,000 English settlers, subsidized by the government in London, arrived in the colony. The long-established Dutch found the English dominance increasingly intolerable and in the mid-thirties began their "Great Trek" into the interior grasslands.

The classic account of this dramatic European trek into the African interior is that of Eric Walker, from whose book the following extracts are taken.

It was not as if the interior were absolutely unknown. Hunters, traders, missionaries, trekboers and reprobates had already gone beyond the Orange, beyond the Vaal, as far as the Limpopo river itself. Eastward a road ran through Kaffirland well-trodden by Wesleyan mission-

From Eric Walker, *The Great Trek* (London: Adam and Charles Black, Ltd., 1934–1960; New York: Barnes & Noble, Inc.), pp. 89–91, 94–97, 101–105. Reprinted by permission of the publishers.

aries and English ivory traders from Port Natal. There was good reason to believe that vast tracts of land in the north and in Natal had been swept clear of native inhabitants by the ferocious Mantatis, Matabele and Zulus.

The Boers knew how to trek. Some of them were trekboers living in their wagons, others were used to trekking once a year from one farm to another. The rest could face it if they must. Already there were men living beyond the borders on all hands, and some of those who still dwelt within the line in the wild northern areas had lived so long in isolation that it was hard to say whether they belonged to the Colony or not. It would be no great matter for such as these to cut the painter altogether. Even in the more established parts of the platteland, the folk were migratory, the *wanderlust* was in their bones. Comparatively few lived in the houses their fathers had built, not many in those in which they themselves had started married life. They were South Africans. Any place in southern Africa where there was good grazing and water would suit them, and from all accounts the land beyond the frontier was better than that within it.

Nevertheless the matter would have to be ripely considered and duly weighed. Landless men and younger sons would, of course, better themselves by trekking. A trek on a big scale, too, would be good fun for the young fellows, a glorified and perpetual picnic. But it was one thing for men to trek thus, and even they would weary of it after a while. To trek with women and children was another matter altogether. It was not so much that family men feared the dangers of a trek on which they would travel in strength. It was that prolonged trekking would come hard on their wives and little ones, and that the mere idea of parting with the home and the bits of things that would have to be left behind would shock their women-folk.

But on broaching the project many Boers found their wives ready and eager to trek. More limited in their interests even than themselves, more vehement, more personal in their ideas and values, it was they who felt and resented most keenly the social revolution that Hottentot equality and slave emancipation were bringing to pass. Their household arrangements were upset. Already Hottentot servants were flitting from one mistress to another, and soon the slaves would be free to flit too; it was harder to control them than it had been. Mantati refugees in the north and stray Fingos in the east did not fill all the gaps and were more incompetent even than Hottentots. Besides, were these coloured folk to compete with their sons for land, to stand on an equality with them before law? It was an outrage to that sense of racial superiority which was naturally stronger in the bearers of children than in the mere begetters of them. Ungodly, that was what it was; "contrary to the laws of God and the natural distinction of race and religion, so that it was intolerable for any decent Christian to bow down beneath such a yoke." Rather than that, leave the Colony for a land somewhere, anywhere, in which Afrikaners could preserve their doctrine of the colour bar in all its purity. Nay, some of them were convinced that it was God's will that they should trek. So it was that many a wife made up her husband's mind for him, or at least made up her own mind to trek before he had quite made up his.

There were leading men in the frontier lands who worked upon this smouldering discontent, notably Gerrit Maritz and Piet Retief. . . .

Maritz and Retief must have found many of their way of thinking. At all events they had the satisfaction of seeing three exploring parties ride out secretly in the middle months of 1834, one north-west, one north, the third due east. If the reports of these *kommissie trekke* were favourable, there would be a trek from the Colony on a large scale. Better than risking a rebellion. Remember Slachter's Nek [where five Boer rebels were hanged in 1815].

The *kommissie trekke* were due to report about the New Year of 1835. Had they reported in time of peace, the Great Trek that followed would, humanly speaking, have been smaller than it actually was, and less bitter in spirit against the Colonial government and the Imperial government that stood behind it. As it was they came back to find the Colony engaged in repelling a Kaffir invasion. Nor was the final and disappointing peace settlement effected till the close of 1836. During those two troubled years, 1835–36, all the old grievances about land and labour and security became more acute, and to them were added new grievances: war losses, the revelation of the financial loss that lay behind the promised slave compensation, and further floods of "unjustifiable odium." It was out of the smoke of burning homesteads and blazing kraals, the stink of gunpowder and blood, the ruin of hopes and the frustration of revenge that the Trekkers went out party by party onto the High Veld.

Everything came together with a rush at the end of 1834 while the *kommissie trekke* were still away on their more or less lawful occasions. First, Dr. Philip appeared on the eastern frontier colloguing with Kaffir chiefs, and Heaven alone knew what he might be saying to them. Then, on the appointed day, the slaves, 39,000 all told, became apprentices to their ex-masters. A few days later the news spread that the Governor had made a treaty with a Griqua chieftain, Andries Waterboer, who, in return for a subsidy and some guns so dangerous in Griqua hands, was to keep order among men of all shades of colour in his stretch of the Orange river valley out to the west of Adam Kok's Philippolis. Finally, just before Christmas, 12,000 Kaffir warriors swept into the Colony on a wide front from the Winterberg to the sea.

The Kaffirs were thrust back by the united efforts of troops, commandos and Hottentots, but not before they had killed 100 white men and coloured men, burned 450 homesteads, and carried off great troops of horses, cattle and sheep. The Colonial forces took full vengeance on warriors and kraals, gardens and herds, and pushed eastwards to the line of the Kei river. Sir Benjamin D'Urban then annexed the country thus traversed under the style of the Province of Queen Adelaide, and sent the commandos home with the promise that the hostile tribes should be expelled therefrom to make way for other occupants.

Here was good news to take home, the prospect of more land, good land. But missionaries and Cape Town philanthropists cried out against this annexation of tribal lands, and the Kaffirs refused obstinately to be "exterminated." They even raided the Colony behind the Governor's back. So out the burghers must come once more at their own expense, to face hardship and deprivation, to develop fresh points of friction with the regulars whose ways were not their ways nor their expressed thoughts on Boer tactics and discipline in any way printable, to see their waggons knocked to pieces and the captured cattle slaughtered troop by troop for rations. And, at the end of it all, the Governor had to agree that the hostile tribes should remain in Queen Adelaide provided they promised to be good subjects of King William. Home the burghers trooped once more, many of them on foot since their horses were dead, labouring under the weight of their great guns.

There was, it is true, still to be some new land as part compensation for the losses and fatigues of the long campaign, land in what was left of the old Ceded Territory, in Queen Adelaide itself and in the Stormberg area farther north which already contained some Boers. At once requests for farms poured in. But prospects of land in these annexed territories paled before the visions of the wonderful new lands beyond the frontiers conjured up by two out of the three *kommissie*. The party that had journeyed north-westward through desperate country into scarcely less desperate Damaraland had to confess that there was no outlet that way. But the second party had pushed north across the mixed karoo and grass-lands of Griqua Philippolis on to splendid grass-lands open and rolling all the way to the Zoutpansberg far beyond Vaal river. As for Piet Uys and his friends who had gone east through Kaffirland to Natal, they admitted that the road was cut across by many rivers and beset by natives, but Natal itself—*Alle wereld!* Where would men find a country like that in all Africa?

The Kaffir war had delayed the Great Trek. Men like Field-Commandant Retief had been too busy leading their burghers to think about it, and even now that the actual fighting was over, trekking on a large scale would be impossible so long as martial law lay heavy on the frontier districts. Nevertheless, in the November of 1835, parties of would-be Trekkers were moving about uneasily just within the north-eastern frontier, and two small groups had actually set out: the first, consisting of Louis Trigardt and his friends from the Kaffir country, the second led by one, Janse van Rensburg, from the far north-eastern confines of the Colony. The Great Trek had begun. . . .

[After the Kaffir War, in 1836, Lieutenant-Governor Stockenstrom set up treaties between the tribesmen and the Boers, but the Boers were no longer interested. They wanted to leave those problems behind. Piet Retief wrote a manifesto of the Trekkers' intentions, the writing of which might be compared to the writing of the Mayflower Compact by pioneers going to America centuries ago, except that Retief's was an affirmation of the old principles now challenged by the British rather than a charter for a new society.—ED.]

Those treaties answered better than frontier tradition would have it, but frontiersmen at the close of 1836 were in no mood to deal with Kaffirs on equal terms nor to put up with checks upon their freedom of action if by any means they could escape them. The British settlers must do the best they could, and so must those Afrikaners who chose to remain in the Old Colony. But the rest could get away from it all by trekking, and now that martial law was gone trekking was easier than it had been. What though the Parliament at Westminster had just passed the Cape of Good Hope Punishment Act subjecting all British citizens south of the twenty-fifth degree of south latitude to the Cape criminal law, that law was useless unless the accused could be brought back within the limits of the Colony. Who was to do that once a man had trekked away beyond the Orange river on to the free soil of the High Veld?

So the Trekkers went drifting out of the tumultuous frontier districts, party by party, all the way around from Algoa Bay to Graaff-Reinet and Beaufort and the Hantam.

They went from mixed motives and with mixed feelings: hopes of better things and of a fresh start, the excitement of adventure, loyalty to the family or the clan, loyalty to the leading local official, fear of isolation when so many of their neighbours were trekking, the dependence of the *bywoner* on his landlord. But the need or desire for new land was very general, and common to all was a determination to live no longer in a colony where the divinely appointed colour bar was so flagrantly disregarded.

Many trekked with little sense of financial loss. Some Trekkers had no farms of their own to leave, and others obtained good prices either in money or in much-needed equipment from English speculators and Afrikaner neighbours with an eye on the possibilities of woolled sheep; good prices, that is, if men took into account the fact that many of these farms had been originally free grants and still lacked title-deeds or anything much in the way of improvements.

Again, a good deal of household stuff could be packed on the waggons. One housewife at all events had three waggons, the first loaded with clothes and dress materials and bedding, and the third with groceries, dried fruit and other sweetstuffs, while another presently had to lament the loss of a fine set of chairs when her waggon overturned on the precipitous passes of the Drakensberg. These may have been exceptional cases, but everyone could reckon on taking stools, chests and small tables, beside the ploughs and picks and spades, the seed and the fruit-trees carefully wrapped up, and of course flour, coffee, sugar, tea, clothing materials, salt, tobacco, and anything up to 300 lb. weight of gunpowder. Over and above all that, their horses and cattle and sheep, their real wealth, went with them beside the waggons.

There was, however, the other side to the story. Waggons were narrow. Goods and chattels soon mounted up to a short ton. Much household gear must be left behind by the better-to-do folk, and many homesteads in which the family had grown up. Prices ranged low on the more exposed parts of the frontier or wherever numbers of farms were thrown on the market together. Some farmers let their places go for an old song, for an apple and an egg as they put it. Some simply left them standing.

All or nearly all of the Trekkers must have felt that the Trek was a great uprooting, and those who did not feel it so at the time came to feel it so in retrospect. Such few writings and still fewer songs as have come down from those days are full of the note of melancholy, of sorrow at parting from old home ties and auld lang syne. It need not all be taken at the foot of the letter. The Trekkers were human and waxed sentimental as most men have done who are "off to Philadelphia in the morning." But when every allowance has been made, the fact remains that unwilling Trekkers felt that the exodus had been forced on them by an unsympathetic government, and the willing found a natural satisfaction in blaming the authorities for making them do what desire and perhaps ambition prompted them to do.

As a community the Trekkers went out of the Old Colony in a state of mind that ranged from a fury of suspicion against the British Government to a dull resentment. They would have no more to do with it or its Colony. They were going up out of the land of Egypt, out of the house of bondage, into the Promised Land. And soon they believed they had found their Moses. Piet Retief had played a man's part in the recent Kaffir war and had earned the friendship of the Governor himself thereby. When he trekked early in 1837 scores went with him and scores followed. The Great Trek which had hitherto been an intermittent trickle became something like a stream.

For later on, when news of disaster came in, bold men hurried off to the rescue, and later still glad tidings of victory encouraged more prudent folk to trek to lands made safe for Afrikaner democracy. In the latest stages of the Great Trek many a man moved off to rejoin his friends and relations. He trekked away from the Colony, home.

Those who trekked with Retief or after him knew for what they were trekking. On the eve of his departure Retief published a manifesto in the *Grahamstown Journal,* the frontier newspaper. That manifesto was at once a confession of faith, a refutation of hostile critics, a programme of reform and a call to action. "As we desire to stand high in the estimation of our brethren," Retief wrote, seeking to put the Trekkers right with themselves and the world, "be it known *inter alia* that we are resolved, wherever we go, that we will uphold the just principle of liberty; but whilst we will take care that no one shall be in a state of slavery, it is our determination to maintain such regulations as may suppress crime and preserve proper relations between master and servant. . . . We will not molest any people, nor deprive them of the smallest property; but, if attacked, we shall consider ourselves fully justified in defending our persons and effects to the utmost of our ability. . . . We propose . . . to make known to the native tribes our intentions, and our desire to live in peace and friendly intercourse with them. . . . We quit this Colony under the full assurance that the English Government has nothing more to require of us, and will allow us to govern ourselves without interference in future."

There it all was, unmistakably: a frontier society, an Afrikaner republic, full forty years after the fall of republican Swellendam and Graaff-Renet. Much of the subsequent history of southern Africa has been a commentary on Piet Retief's manifesto.

[But neither the Great Trek nor the government-encouraged emigration from England enticed any significant follow-up migration. Pay for agricultural work was low, determined by the rates for Hottentot and Kaffir labor, and this discouraged the migration of crofters and farm laborers from Europe. The mass migration went to North America instead of to South Africa, which thus missed the stimulus of immigrant competition and fresh ideas and became only more rigid in its economic and racial philosophy—Ed.]

IV / ASIAN MIGRATION

Asia, most densely peopled of all the continents, also has been the scene of vast population movements—largely because density itself has forced men to seek their livelihood elsewhere. Not dramatic armed hordes, but the persistent infiltration of laborers and merchants, is what has carried Chinese blood and culture abroad—to Southeast Asia, Formosa, Hawaii, and North and South America. Similarly, the Japanese have expanded into neighboring islands and across the Pacific, until their Great East Asian Co-Prosperity Sphere collapsed in World War II. The Indians have migrated largely to Southeast Asia and to East Africa, where in many communities they have become the dominant trading element.

But the massive population base of these peoples has frightened the Australians, the Canadians, the Americans, and others, who have more land space but fear being inundated. The Asians' differences in appearance and customs, their industry and apparent humility, and their tendency to concentrate into their own communities have encouraged discrimination against them, especially in race-conscious lands. Hence the potential flood has been restrained, but at the expense of bitter resentment. Their own internal animosities, as between the Indians and the Pakistani, only accentuate the tragedy in the story of Asian migration, though there are bright spots, too, as in the peaceful co-existence that characterizes the Asian-Caucasian mixing bowl in Hawaii.

22 / ASIA ON THE MOVE

Some sense of the extent and variety of Asian migration may be had through these excerpts from the broad factual survey by Bruno Lasker.

One may note also within Asia itself the parallels to the opposition to immigration so well known in the United States and in Australia— witness the Burmese antagonism to Indian immigration.

Lasker deals with situations up to the end of World War II. Despite later movements, such as the great Chinese influx into Taiwan, basic problems and attitudes remain fundamentally the same.

In the history of eastern Asia, international migration has usually been short-range migration. Only in modern times has it mastered longer distances and taken advantage of striking differences in economic opportunity. For millions of peasants, all travel beyond the hills visible on the horizon still is "foreign" migration—in the sense that, as soon as he has left the small realm dominated by his own ethnic group, the migrant is treated as a stranger and feels a stranger.

Increasingly, artificial patterns of political division—in the East as in the West—have accentuated the distinction between domestic and foreign travel. A century ago, a merchant from Amoy may have felt more at home in Manila than in Shanghai. Today he can be in no doubt as to where he is a citizen and where an alien. The earlier international migrations, if they were not connected with wars of conquest, represented intensifications of more tenuous relations previously established. Typical colonists are the soldiers left behind to guard a frontier or a newly acquired territorial possession, and the member of a merchant family left behind at a foreign trading depot to check on deliveries and to prepare shipments. But today international migration in eastern Asia has all the complications of a four-sided tournament. In the receiving country one party uses proven devices to attract the immigrant, another raises barriers to keep him out. In the country of origin, some make it their business to push sedent farmers out into the unknown—labor, as the largest "export commodity" of southern China, has become big business—and others to hold them back. The attitude that there is something rather immoral about leaving one's village has not died out. But the numbers involved in foreign migration are still relatively small. The movements of greatest numerical importance are those of Chinese to the countries of the *Nan Yang* (the South Seas in the literal geographical sense) and to Manchuria; of Koreans to Manchuria and Japan; of Japanese to Manchuria, Malaya, Netherlands

Bruno Lasker, *Asia on the Move* (New York: Henry Holt and Co., 1945). (Issued under the auspices of the American Council, Institute of Pacific Relations). Pp. 57–93 passim. Reprinted by permission of the author and publisher.

India, and the Philippines; of Filipinos to the United States; of Indians to Burma and British Malaya.

There have also in pre-depression years been a number of minor movements of migration in eastern Asia, most of them continuous over long periods: Indians to Thailand; Javanese to British Malaya, British Borneo, and New Caledonia; Annamites to various Pacific island groups; Filipinos to South China, Thailand, Indo-China, and Japan; Chinese to and from Hong Kong, Macao, and Formosa.

Indian

There are two forms of Indian migration to Malaya, assisted and un-assisted. The latter group, composed in recent prewar years more often of voluntary labor migrants than formerly, when it was composed entirely of merchants, rose from 12 per cent of the total in 1920 to 38 per cent in 1934, 87 per cent in 1936, 89 per cent (another published statement says, probably in error, 48 per cent) in 1937, and 79 per cent in 1938. Although improvement in labor conditions may have something to do with these proportions, they reflect in the main an improvement in trade after the depression. The Controller of Labour attributes the rising proportion of unassisted migrants in the total to the desire of laborers to escape the week's quarantine imposed on those assisted by the planters. Many thousands of indentured laborers were repatriated during the depression.

The Indian government also had supervisory rights over Indians employed on contract labor in Thailand and Burma. In both of these countries larger numbers of Indian immigrants were artisans and merchants. Exact statistics concerning the Indian residents in Thailand are not available. In 1934, their number was estimated as about one hundred thousand, and with the growing antagonism this figure probably did not rise appreciably through fresh immigration when trade recovered.

In Burma, over a million of the country's sixteen million inhabitants spoke an Indian language. How many of these were first-generation or recent immigrants is not known. On the other hand, many thousands of descendants of Indian immigrants undoubtedly are included among the ten million who, in the census returns of 1931, gave Burmese as their mother tongue. For, with the growing unpopularity of their own group, many of the second and third generation of immigrants would be likely to identify themselves with the dominant group. According to a report by a British medical officer in the Indian Civil Service, more than seven hundred thousand Indians passed through the mountain passes on foot in 1942 to regain their home country. Two hundred a day were being evacuated by plane in the spring of 1942.

In 1938 and 1939, an anti-foreign agitation that had been going on for some years, led to a riot against Indian Moslems, in the course of which two hundred persons were killed and large losses of property were incurred. The Indian residents had long been disliked in Burma much for the same reason that Chinese are disliked in many parts of Southeast Asia, namely because they are sharp traders and usurers.

In July, 1941, an agreement was published by the governments of India and Burma regulating and restricting the admission of Indians to Burma.

It was intended to remove from Burmans reasonable apprehension that Burma might be subjected to undue economic competition by reason of such immigration, while securing for Indians settled in Burma recognition of their proper rights. The principles underlying the agreement were that Burma had the right to determine the composition of her population, and that Indians who have wholly identified themselves with the interests of Burma should enjoy the same rights as members of her permanent population. The agreement has been strongly attacked by Indian nationalists, led by Mr. Gandhi, who urged among other points that public opinion had been inadequately consulted, and that the measure cast a slur upon Indians

Filipino

Concerning Filipino emigration little need be said because there is so little. The population is very unevenly distributed over the archipelago; but there is little inducement to move off to the surrounding countries because labor conditions in the Philippines, poor as they are, still are better than those elsewhere in that region. There has been neither much desire to emigrate, other than to the United States, nor active recruiting. In recent years, even migration to Hawaii and continental United States has been frowned upon by the Philippine government, partly from pride, partly to avoid friction, and partly because there is not really any reason why those able agricultural workers whom the American employers desire should not help to develop their own country. Systematic settlement of Mindanao, through the establishment of agricultural colonies by the government, started in 1913. The earlier experiments, however, proved too costly, and in 1918 the Inter-Island Migration Division was established to recruit a more suitable personnel for homesteading in selected thinly populated parts of that large island. By 1934, some six thousand pioneer families had been settled with government assistance and another thirty thousand or so had been sent under the auspices of other agencies. All this proved much too slow to accomplish the object of developing Mindanao with the aid of pioneer settlers, and in 1939 a National Land Settlement Administration was established to set up a limited number of large colonies designed on a community basis. There had not, of course, been time enough at the time of the Japanese occupation to permit of a thorough appraisal of these schemes; but some of their technical inadequacies had already become sufficiently apparent to produce plans for improvements. . . .

How many Filipinos are there in the United States? The returns of the 1940 census show that there has been no change in ten years. In 1930, we had 45,208 Filipinos in continental United States; in 1940 there were 45,563. Although the same in number, the Filipinos in the United States are less conspicuous than they were. More of them have become fully assimilated. The adult age level has gone up, and there is also a larger proportion of children. The number of young Filipinos engaged in commercial agriculture as laborers has decreased considerably.*

Objectively considered (which it rarely was), the number of Filipino residents in the United States never was large, in relation either to Philippine population pressure or to American labor requirements. It may be taken for granted that there will be no renewal of Filipino labor immigration to the United States, even when restrictions of a racially discriminatory character will have been removed from our immigration law. (Under the Independence Act of 1934, an annual quota of fifty Filipino immigrants to continental United States is permitted until 1946.) Employers on the Pacific Coast have become reconciled to the use of Mexican labor, the inflow of which can be better regulated in relation to cyclical and seasonal variations in demand. In Hawaii, the number of resident Filipinos dropped from about 70,000 in 1930 to 52,000 in 1940; but most of these are now permanent residents. Active labor recruiting in the Philippines stopped some years ago, and the movement of laborers between Manila and Honolulu has assumed very small proportions.

The only other country where numbers of Filipino immigrants are to be seen is, curiously enough, China. They are members of Chinese-Filipino families with residences or connections in both countries.

* By 1960, however, the U.S. Census showed 201,746 Filipinos in the United States, of whom 104,843 were born abroad. The 1960 figure, of course, included Hawaii.

Under the pressure of increased anti-Chinese feeling in the Islands, nationalism among Chinese-Filipinos grew strongly in the early thirties. Thus, when China was invaded, and even before, thousands of Filipinos with Chinese parents or grandparents went to China to study or to engage in business. While there, they were under the protection of American consuls, until they had to leave, as subjects of the United States.

Emigration from Southern China

We turn, then, to the much larger and more complicated subject of Chinese emigration. It started as an overflow. People were literally shoved off the shores into the sea. Some groups colonized such islands as Formosa and Hainan. Some, deprived of the right to own land, stayed on the water and still live by the tens of thousands on their boats.

For many generations, a stream of migrants poured uninterruptedly from the two southernmost provinces of China, Kwangtung and Fukien, many of them as merchant adventurers, some to return after long voyages, some to stay abroad. They were intrenched in Malacca before the coming of the Portuguese, in the Philippines before the coming of the Spaniards, in the Indian Archipelago before the coming of the British and the Dutch. The Nan Yang, or South Seas, has remained their favorite destination. There they were for centuries a master race, not coolies.

The large increase in the number and size of large-scale foreign enterprises in the Asiatic tropics in the first quarter of the present century brought with it a corresponding increase in Chinese immigration, but it also set going, in times of business depression, a reverse movement, until the migrations back and forth came to resemble more the short-term labor migrations between European countries or between Mexico and the United States than the old-time Chinese migration for a period of contract labor as a first step toward permanent settlement overseas. This does not mean that contract workers do not still try to stay if conditions are favorable, but it has become more difficult for them. Their own consul sees to it that they do not hang around when out of work—on the chance that, as business improved, they might either get their job back or join some townsman in the establishment of a small business. There is more travel back and forth, and more members of the same family take part in it. There has also, in recent prewar years, been a noteworthy increase in the emigration of Chinese women—a movement now often encouraged by estate employers because it keeps their Chinese male workers happier and because it provides them with a supply of cheap and unexpectedly efficient labor if managed with a little finesse.

Corresponding to these changes, migration between Southeast Asia and southern China has become much more sensitive to fluctuations in business activity. Larger proportions of contract laborers and other emigrants return home after two or three years with little to show for their work abroad, although, while it lasted, it helped to support their families. Another result of this short-range migration experience has been a lessening of social distance between the emigrants and the stay-at-homes. Instead of arriving as "rich uncles" whose wishes must be obeyed if their benefactions to family and home community are to continue (sometimes they do get tired of their relatives and retire to a modern house in the nearest city, or even to Hong Kong or Shanghai), the returned emigrant of the new class remains "one of the boys"; and while he may not have changed much in his tastes and ideas, since he had little opportunity to get away from his Chinese labor gang, when he does dilate on the values of modern hygiene or a schooling, he is listened to with attention. Another consequence of the increased mobility is that even the older, partly assimilated Chinese colonies abroad have been brought into closer touch with the political and economic life of China.

With the beginning of the world economic depression in the late 'twenties, as in previous business depressions, the normal excess of Chinese emigration overseas over return migration was reversed. In 1930 over half a million workers were forced by the economic depression to return to their homeland, in 1931 almost three hundred thousand. Anti-Chinese movements gained force in Thailand, Burma, Netherlands India, and the Philippines. Thousands of independent Chinese colonists—farmers, artisans, small business men, and wage earners—bought steamship tickets home; and other thousands were repatriated under the terms of their contract. There were also many, especially descendants of mixed marriages who previously had considered themselves Chinese, who now silently disappeared into the general citizenry of their adopted country (in Thailand, more especially).

Hostility to Chinese residents in Burma was less pronounced than that to Indians, although the former had, in the decade 1920 to 1930, increased twice as fast. The reason is that the Chinese, many of them married to Burmese wives and assimilated to Burmese ways, had become essential to the country's commerce and industry, took little part in politics, and offered a counterpart of ties with a neighboring power to the involuntary ties with India and the British Empire. With the building of the Burma Road and the beginning of the Burma-Yunan Railroad in 1938 and 1939, and especially with the accumulating evidences of the Chinese government's intention to settle and develop the frontier region, old fears long latent revived.

Actually, the number of Chinese residents in Rangoon in 1941 was no more than 36,556, only about 6,000 more than in 1931. At that time the Chinese minority of Burma consisted of 194,000 persons, two-thirds of them male, about one-third of them living close to the Chinese border in the Shan and Wa States. The importance of the group lay in the part they played in the non-agricultural sector of Burma's economy. They made up almost one-fourth of the miners, one-tenth of those engaged in trade, in banking, in metalwork, in hotel and restaurant services. They also were popular in such professions as dentistry.

Korea

Like other Asiatic peninsulas, Korea has a long history of immigration and emigration. It was populated from the north and from China to the west. Its fertile southern lowlands attracted would-be conquerors from every direction, but for many centuries it managed to carry on a precarious independent existence. In its turn it helped to civilize Japan, to which it gave many of those arts which are now cherished by that country's panegyrists as characteristic fruits of the native genius. It also sent forth an occasional population surplus to people some of the fertile valleys beyond its northern mountain frontier and to extend its fishing into northern waters. The growth of population did not keep within the bounds set by the country's natural resources and the state of the people's arts. Famine and pestilence took their toll.

Since 1910, the internal and external migrations of Korea have been dominated by brutal conquest. In the first decade of Japanese occupation, hundreds of thousands of Korean farmers were squeezed from the best arable land to less and less desirable land and, many of them, off the land altogether. Those who did not become tenant farmers for Japanese landlords were forced to submit as wage-earners to the humiliating labor conditions imposed on them by Japanese employers. And more than a million of them became the pawns of Japan's expansionist policy in Manchuria and North China. This controlled movement of migration was used not only for economic purposes, but also to clear out of Korea as much as possible of the element active in opposition to Japanese rule.

Manchuria benefited from the distress of native farming in Korea under Japanese sovereignty since 1910 by a steady influx of agricultural immigrants who have done much to improve the land in the provinces of Chien Tao and Kirin. Jurisdiction over these immigrants, first only in the South Manchuria Railway Zone but later in all parts of Manchuria, was one of the hottest objects of dispute between Japan and China ever since 1910. In 1909, the Tumen River had been recognized as the boundary between China and Korea, and an area in the Chien Tao district had been opened up for Korean colonization, with the proviso that the Korean immigrants were to submit to the laws of China. With the annexation of Korea, however, Japan claimed that these emigrants were subjects of the Mikado and entitled to the "protection" of extraterritoriality and consular jurisdiction. By the Sino-Japanese Treaty of 1915, most of the rights which the Japanese claimed were conceded; they included the permission of unlimited immigration and leasing of land on the part of Koreans. After that, the Korean emigrant farmers more and more became Japan's cat's-paws in continued pressure on China.

23 / "THE BIRTH OF TWO NATIONS"— THE INDIAN-PAKISTANI EXCHANGE AFTER WORLD WAR II

Among the great "forced migrations" or exchanges of population that between India and Pakistan could hardly be called typical, for each of these movements is a case apart; nor is the example typical of Asian migration. Yet it all happened in Asia and reflects the Asian situation. This migration and counter-migration illustrate, therefore, something of the problems of Asia as well as the inevitable difficulties in the transfer of vast numbers of people—the personal suffering, the contrast between expectation and realization, the contributory natural disasters that exacerbate the tragedies of change, the economic disruption in industry and agriculture caused by the sudden drawing of new boundaries, the hatreds and fears enhanced by uncertainty.

Margaret Bourke-White, world-famous photographer, here draws word pictures of this massive flight, pictures as vivid as those she captured on film.

With the coming of independence to India, the world had the chance to watch a most rare event in the history of nations: the birth of twins.

Excerpted from Margaret Bourke-White, *Interview with India* (London: Phoenix House, Ltd., 1950), pages 15–22. [Published in the United States as *Halfway to Freedom* (Simon and Schuster)]. Used by permission of Laurence Pollinger, Ltd., and Simon and Schuster. Copyright © 1949 by Margaret Bourke-White.

It was a birth accompanied by strife and suffering, but I consider myself fortunate to have witnessed and been able to document the historic early days of these two nations: India and Pakistan.

When I went to the Punjab area, in the North of India, in the autumn of 1947 to begin photographing the new-born sovereign states, massive exchange of populations was under way. The roads connecting the Union of India with Pakistan looked as Oxford Street or the Charing Cross Road look during the rush hour. But instead of the two-way stream of motor-cars there were endless convoys of bullock carts, women on donkey back, men on foot carrying on their shoulders the very young or the very old.

Babies were born along the way. People died along the way. Some died of cholera, some from the attacks of hostile religious communities. But many of them simply dropped out of line from sheer weariness and sat by the roadside to wait patiently for death. Sometimes I saw children pulling at the arms and hands of a parent or grandparent, unable to comprehend that those arms would never be able to carry them again. The name "Pakistan" means Land of the Pure: many of the pure never got there. The way to their Promised Land was lined with graves.

The hoofs of countless cattle raised such continuous columns of dust that a pillar of a cloud trailed the convoys by day. And in the evenings when the wayfarers camped by tens of thousands along the roadsides, and built their little fires and made their chapatties—a good deal, I suppose, like the unleavened bread of the Bible—the light of their camp fires rose into the dust-filled air until it seemed as if a pillar of fire hung over them at night. . . .

They flowed in a two-way stream across the border. Into the Indian Union came the Hindus and Sikhs (differing slightly in their religious practice, the warlike Sikhs, famous for their picturesque beards and turbans, are an offshoot of the Hindu religion); the Muslims poured into their new Pakistan, which they looked on as their Promised Land. All were led by fear, by highly questionable leadership, by ever dwindling hope. What had been merely arbitrarily drawn areas on a map began emptying and refilling with human beings—neatly separated into so-called "opposite" religious communities—as children's crayons fill in an outline map in geography class. But this was no child's play. This was a massive exercise in human misery.

As though the travail of a people divided by pen strokes was not great enough, North India, in this year of all years, suffered the worst floods since 1900. . . . The River Beas claimed the most victims. When the water began receding sufficiently for me to get to it, I photographed one meadow between the river and a railway ramp where four thousand Muslims had gone in to camp for the night. Only one thousand had come out alive. That meadow was like a battlefield: carts overturned wildly, household goods and farm tools pressed into a mash of mud and wreckage. Several nights later I chanced on an encampment of the survivors of the Beas disaster just as they were settling down for the night. I talked with one man who was digging a grave by the side of the road. His name was Rasik; he came from Jullundur, where he and his brothers had owned a ten-acre orange grove. The grave was for his eight-year-old son, who had died just that afternoon. Rasik had been carrying the child's body until he had a chance to bury it properly and recite prayers over the grave, as any father would wish to do. . . .

More fearful than flood and starvation was the ever-present threat of attack by hostile religious hordes along the way. Hatreds had been so whipped up by the political pressures which had divided the nations that a new morality had developed. All members of a different religious group were fair prey for loot and murder. Travel by train was still more dangerous than by road because of the ease with which a crowded refugee train could be switched off the main tracks and, while being shunted back and forth, attacked and looted. The railway station in Amritsar was a place of dread for Muslims. Amritsar, the holy city of the Sikhs and therefore the centre of an especially militant form of fanaticism, was the last big junction which Muslim refugee trains had to pass through before crossing into Pakistan. I remember visiting the frightfully littered railway station after an attack which had cost the lives of a thousand Muslim refugees, and seeing a row of dignified-looking Sikhs, venerable in their long beards and wearing the bright blue turbans of the militant Akali sect, sitting cross-legged all along the platform. Each patriarchal figure held a long curved sabre across his knees—waiting quietly for the next train. The Muslims were not always the victims. Trainloads of Sikhs and Hindus emigrating to India had hours of equal dread when passing through Lahore, the last great rail junction before they escaped from Pakistan. Hindu-Sikh convoys on the Pakistan highroads were a constant temptation to Muslim raiders. . . .

No matter where these Muslim peasants had lived in India, they knew exactly where they wanted to live in Pakistan. Everybody wanted a farm in Lyallpur. There is no richer land in the whole Indian sub-continent, and when the national dividing line was drawn between the East and West Punjab, Lyallpur fell in Pakistan. Less than thirty years ago the Lyallpur district had been wilderness. Then it was settled by the Sikhs. In addition to being the most warlike people of India, this fiercely independent Hindu sect also makes the sturdiest farmers. Having received this acreage of jungle as a premium for fighting in the first World War, the Sikhs cleared the forests, dug canals, and tilled the fields. Within a single generation they had begun reaping rich harvests of wheat, cotton, and oilseeds, and had built their strong-walled villages, each centred around its sacred gurdwara in which they gathered to worship their one God. . . .

Those who left the Lyallpur district were particularly stunned by their swift eviction. In this group of villages, Muslims made up only 25 to 40 per cent of the population and had always lived on com-radely terms with the Sikh farmers. When bloodshed started in sur-rounding districts, their Muslim neighbors said, "There will be no trouble here. We have been living here as brothers." But the hatreds which had been unleashed to achieve partition could not be caged; rather, they ran wild when division on religious lines became a reality. Isolated peasant groups were powerless to resist the stampede of terror.

I remember Gurdit Singh, who told me how the crisis grew. Gurdit Singh and his brothers and brothers' wives were part of a gigantic convoy with its thousands of ox-drawn carts packed muzzle to wheel in a solidly moving column eighteen miles long. I had a chance to talk with them when they were halted on the road by a broken cart wheel. I had stopped to watch the desperate drama of fixing the wheel, the cart top-heavy with its creaking load of bicycles, bedding, farm tools, and frying pans, and the men straining at the wagon shaft, looking like some strange breed of earth giants with their beards and hairy arms and eyebrows caked with dust and angry flies in whirling clouds around their heads. When the cart was mended they paused for a few moments and told me of the sudden terror that had descended on their village.

The first night it was just a small knot of Muslims who gathered in the sugar-cane field outside their village wall, and shouted, 'Come out. Come out.' But the next night their entire village was ringed with Muslims who must have come from far off, since they outnumbered those in their own neighbourhood. By midnight the air was frightening with their cries of *'Allah ho Akbar'* ('God is great')—the battle cry of the Muslims. As the Sikhs mounted anxious watch on their rooftops, they could see a red glow on the horizon which told them other villages were being sacked and burned. Just before dawn, the Muslim schoolmaster slipped through the lines. 'Do not leave,' he said. 'We Mussulmans have always lived in peace with you here in Lyallpur. We will protect you. We will die with you.' But the next night the beating of a large drum sounded from the sugar cane. This, the Sikhs knew, was the signal of attack. The skyline was vivid with fires, and at midnight the schoolteacher came again. 'We cannot help now,' he said, and he wept as he delivered a written ultimatum which he, as the most literate member of the community, had been instructed to write out. It read: 'This is our country. You must go away. You may not take any movable property as the land and the property belong to Pakistan.'

Knowing that a large convoy was forming at Beloki Head, the villagers sent a request at dawn to the town hall, asking for an escort to start them on their way. The District Magistrate sent soldiers to protect them while they loaded whatever belongings their carts would carry. Then he sealed their houses in the hope of keeping out looters, and provided an escort for the Sikhs as they left to join the great exodus toward the Indian Union.

With regret the District Magistrate, himself a Muslim, watched these expert Sikh tillers go. It would take some time before the incoming refugees, who had grown up in another type of agriculture, would develop comparable skill in handling the irrigation channels and spillways. Already the cycle of harvest and planting had been disrupted throughout the entire area where populations were being exchanged. Delay in the next crop would intensify the coming food shortage, inevitable with the ever-growing flood of refugees.

24 / AUSTRALIA AND THE RESTRICTION OF ASIAN IMMIGRATION

Problems of racial and cultural mixing, of the relative importance of economic and strategic factors, and of all the interconnected political aspects of these questions are not confined to the United States. In each country the details of problems and their solutions vary; yet the same issues of human relationships may be seen in diverse places.

A. T. Yarwood, *Asian Migration to Australia. The Background to Exclusion 1896–1923.* Melbourne: Melbourne University Press, 1964, reissued 1967. Reprinted by permission of Cambridge University Press.

*Especially striking are the similarities between the United States,
South Africa, and Australia. The basic difficulties are well summed up
by A. T. Yarwood, a senior lecturer in history at the University of
New South Wales. In his book Yarwood surveys the colonial background, the restriction act of 1901, and the specific problems of Japanese, Chinese, Indian, and Syrian immigration. In his conclusion,
here reproduced in its entirety, he makes plain why Australia, a land
whose development was dependent upon immigration, stood firm in its
purpose of giving structure to the nation while also slowly modifying
its earlier contempt for non-white races.*

Two principles emerged in the late colonial period that were to guide
Commonwealth action on the restriction of Asian immigration. The
first, enunciated by Joseph Chamberlain, was that exclusive legislation
should be non-discriminatory in form, at least so far as it affected races
in which Britain had special interest, notably the Indians and the Japanese. Reminded of this requirement by the Colonial Secretary's des-
patch explaining the reasons for disallowing the Queensland Sugar
Works Guarantee Act the Australian Prime Minister committed his
government to the "education test." He persisted in this decision in
spite of hostile criticism from the Labor and Free Trade Parties and
from within the ranks of his own supporters. The eventual passage of
his Bill probably owed much to a realization that the viability of a
"White Australia" depended on British naval protection. This was a
humiliating position for Australian nationalists to accept, and it was
largely with the aim of creating a greater measure of self-dependence
that a programme of military and naval defence was laid down towards the end of the Commonwealth's first decade.

The second principle, very much the product of George Reid's
statesmanship, and emphatically vindicated by the experience of
Queensland and later of the United States, was that a foothold should
be denied to the subjects of an Asian power which might take up the
cudgels on behalf of its distressed nationals. In 1901 Edmund Barton
showed not the slightest inclination to yield to Japan's persistent
requests that her subjects should be exempted from the Act. Subsequently, for all his anxiety to achieve harmonious relations with
Japan, Alfred Deakin was constrained to refuse the right of settlement
to Japanese.

By the time the Immigration Restriction Bill had completed its
progress through the Senate it had been given the grudging support of
the Labor Party as the best available measure for dealing with Asian

immigration. With the choice of any European language left to the discretion of the officer, the test had a potential severity and flexibility which recommended it to this party, representing as it did groups in the community that had most to lose from an influx of Asian labourers. Within a few weeks of the Act's coming into force it had become apparent that Labor parliamentarians were assuming the responsibility of ensuring that its potential was fully realized. When occupying the cross-benches they probed administrative deficiencies and drew attention to loopholes in the law through which a number of Asians had gained admission. Probably as a result of this continuous pressure, effective because it was exerted by a party holding the balance of power, the Protectionist government modified the test so that it took on a really prohibitive character. When in power Labor initiated an impressive number of legislative and administrative measures that were designed to frustrate the attempts of Chinese to enter Australia il·licitly by stowing away, deserting and by using false papers. A comparison of the records of various governments during our period leaves no doubt as to the special role of the Labor Party as the guardian of the ports.

"A nation for a continent, and a continent for a nation." This was a saying that had popular currency during the nineties, expressing a belief in the unique opportunity offered to the people of the Australian colonies, then in the process of forming themselves into a nation. Significantly, the first non-machinery Act passed by the Parliament of the federated colonies was one aimed at seizing this opportunity by preventing the growth within the nation of racial cleavages far more inimical to political stability and social harmony than the divisions that had been brought substantially to an end by the Constitution Act of 1900.

The policy of protectionism that was increasingly favoured by the Commonwealth involved the sacrifice of economy and efficiency in the name of definite public goals. Similarly, the policy of excluding coloured labourers implied the acceptance of a limited rate of national development, especially in the tropical areas, as a reasonable price to pay for racial homogeneity. This strong element of national self-denial was well brought out by the *Sydney Morning Herald's* dictum that: "no commercial benefits that we could conceive would be commensurate with the evils that might come upon Australia from an unrestricted influx of Asiatics." It was expressed in rather more terse language by Prime Minister Barton in response to the deputation of shipping representatives who appealed vainly for relief from the provisions of the Bill that threatened their interests. Examples may be multiplied of the consequences of this policy: the repatriation of the Kanakas and the payment of a bounty for "white" grown sugar; the white labour clause in the Post and Telegraph Act and its consequential increase in the costs of mail contracts; and generally, the rejection of the easy profits and the rapid utilization of tropical resources that might have been facilitated by the importation of coloured workers.

While making a very special and limited exception of the pearl-shelling industry, the Commonwealth maintained an inflexible stand on the question of indentured coloured labour. The millions of words written by its advocates and opponents rather obscure the fact that at no time during our period was it a live political issue in Australia. No political party nor even any party leader in the Federal Parliament challenged the belief that the preservation of racial homogeneity must remain a fundamental aim of Australian governments. For this reason it is not considered necessary to examine in detail the heterodoxy of some conservative journals and newspapers, of indiscreet State Governors, of one State Premier, of the Associated Chambers of Commerce and of a few federal backbenchers, whose arguments had no effect either on the basic policy or on its detailed administration, except perhaps to indicate the existence of an element that did not share the general aim.

Most of those who urged the admission of coloured labourers claimed that their proposals would in no way infringe the "White Australia" policy. Indeed, they commonly held that the policy applied by the Commonwealth was self-destructive, and that in the absence of coolie labour, allegedly uniquely suited to tropical work as well as cheap, the northern parts of the continent must languish undeveloped and unpopulated. According to this line of reasoning the established policy was not only morally reprehensible, in that it transgressed some supposed obligation for a nation to exploit its resources at a maximum rate, but also strategically unsound as it left the "richest unoccupied area of the globe" an inviting bait to invasion by the overpopulated countries of Asia. A "well regulated system" of indentured coloured labour could disarm Asian critics, create supervisory jobs for Australian workers and profits for Australian capitalists, and at the same time establish an effective barrier against potential aggressors. Common to such plans was an insistence that the coolies should be admitted on condition of compulsory repatriation, their movements restricted to an area north of a "colour line" drawn, perhaps, through the Tropic of

Capricorn, permanently disqualified from political rights and forbidden to aspire to occupations that suited the white man.

Not a single feature of these proposals escaped criticism by orthodox exponents of the "White Australia" policy. Most of all they offended the prevailing belief in the dignity of labour, which implied the rejection of a society in which certain kinds of work should be reserved for a menial race or class. The old assumptions about the population-carrying capacity of northern Australia and about the special fitness of the coloured races for manual labour in the tropics no longer went unchallenged by scientists and publicists. It was pointed out that Australia's security would in no way be enhanced by the presence of a mass of unassimilated aliens whose loyalties to the governing race must be suspect. Even if it were true that white men could not live, work and breed in the tropics, there would be less danger in preserving the *status quo* than in deliberately creating a situation comparable with that of the southern states of America, of South Africa, of Kenya or of Fiji.

Although the Northern Territory proved no more attractive to white settlers after the assumption of control by the Commonwealth in 1911, there was no sign of a rethinking of Australian attitudes to coloured labour. In February 1915 the Governor of South Australia expressed his opinion of the climatic limitations on the employment of white manual workers, and hinted that the loyalty of Indian troops in the war might receive a tangible reward in the form of labour recruitment for the Australian tropics. The speech aroused angry protests from the Prime Minister, who described it as a "grave official indiscretion" on the part of a representative of the Crown, while the *Bulletin* commented that "No more unsuitable moment could possibly be chosen for controversy on this subject." The Adelaide *Register* congratulated Governor Galway on having courageously and intelligently espoused a doctrine that it had been preaching for years, but the weight of newspaper opinion agreed with the Sydney *Daily Telegraph* that "The determination of the Australian people is to preserve this continent for the white race . . . the national confidence in the soundness of this principle is too well grounded to justify a belief that there will be any surrender." At the same time Galway's right to express an opinion was defended against the "touchiness" of the Labor Prime Minister.

The Australian public was not alone in its emphatic rejection of such proposals. Unofficial members of the Indian Legislative Council had campaigned against the indentured labour system, which was suspended by regulation in 1917 and abolished by the Emigration Act of 1922. In Britain there had been a marked growth of sympathy for the problems of the scantily-populated white dominions, as evidenced by the statements of Colonel Seely and Earl Crewe. The sentiments of *The Times* in 1901 had been conveyed in tendentious reports and editorials that interpreted Australian immigration legislation as being inspired by the excessively powerful Labor Party in defence of its own narrow interests. From 1907 its comments on Australia's policy reflected an awareness of the critical nature of the domestic and international crises then developing over racial questions in South Africa and between the United States and Japan. An editorial in 1922 frankly applauded the "White Australia" policy which it now regarded as being aimed at preserving race purity. In short, the examples of race problems in other parts of the world served not only to confirm Australian policy but also to convince some erstwhile critics of its essential virtue.

The race consciousness that underlay the "White Australia" policy underwent some changes during the passage of the years. In 1901 the desire for racial homogeneity manifested itself in expressions of intolerance and superiority towards the coloured races, described by Prime Minister Barton as being intrinsically inferior to the whites. By the end of our period Australian publicists and politicians explicitly disavowed the suggestion that the "White Australia" policy was based on assumptions of race superiority. They referred instead to differences between Oriental and European cultures, which militated against their fusion into one harmonious society. The change of emphasis may be ascertained by comparing the *Bulletin's* denigration of Japan in 1904 with its recognition in 1919 of the "distinction of the Japanese, their force and their intellectual gifts."

This development involved something far deeper than a mere tactical desire to placate a powerful Pacific neighbour. The achievements of the Japanese people in the first two decades of the twentieth century had acted as a striking rebuttal of the doctrine of the inferiority of the coloured races. More generally, as an Australian observer remarked in a *Round Table* article, the contraction of the Asian minorities in Australia had removed a prime cause of race friction and had made for a lessening of the prejudice exhibited towards them. The success of the Act of 1901 had cleared the way for the more equitable treatment of resident Asians and for the progressive liberalization of the temporary entry policy.

The administrative history of the period under review may be summed up in terms of two concurrent developments: the easing of conditions for temporary entry; and the strengthening of the Act's provisions against evasion. Policy varied significantly from one Asian race to another. In its determination, reference was made to the needs of foreign, imperial and, to a much lesser degree, commercial relations. Of importance domestically were the size of the resident Asian group and the nature of its relations with the public (especially with the Labor movement) and with the Department. Labor and non-Labor Ministers tended to adopt different approaches to the detailed administration of policy, the latter being rather more susceptible to the claims of individuals to special consideration. But in deciding on major questions, as for example, the permanent entry of the Chinese wives, no government could ignore the desirability of administrative continuity or the necessity of maintaining public confidence.

25 / CHINESE MIGRATION TO THE UNITED STATES

Out of the vast population reservoir of China men have migrated for centuries, to find less crowded homes and more profitable work. Expansion directed itself at first to neighboring lands, but in the nineteenth century the outpouring of men spread round the world—to Latin America, Africa, Hawaii, the North American mainland, and farther. Chinese labor helped to build the railways of the American West and to dig wealth from mines. San Francisco became a kind of American capital for the Chinese "sojourners" in the United States and still retains its colorful Chinatown. The following passages, however, will describe the less widely known movements from the American West Coast into the mountains and on to the South and the East.

Gunther Barth, a historian who received his doctorate from Harvard and then went to teach at the University of California at Berkeley, has produced a revealing and understanding account of the Chinese migration and of the contemporary reaction to it.

For two decades the boundaries of the mining region in the foothills of the Sierra Nevada were also the limits of Chinese California. That area harbored the mass of sojourners. An invisible control system, sustained

Reprinted by permission of the publishers from Gunther Barth, *Bitter Strength: A History of the Chinese in the U. S., 1850–70.* Cambridge, Mass.: Harvard University Press, Copyright, 1964, by the President and Fellows of Harvard College. This excerpt has been taken from pp. 183–89, 196–202, 212–13.

by devotion to the family, permeated this isolated world. Neither strife nor acculturation fundamentally weakened the controls of the clan organizations, district companies, tongs, and guilds.

Other factors, however, stimulated the movement of Chinese into the Rocky Mountains, the South, and the East and helped demolish the oppressive control system. The national diffusion of the problem expedited acculturation, facilitated by the discovery, through personal contact, of the Chinese as individuals.

The problem became national as a result of the sojourners' outward movement. Labor companies brought the newcomers to the South and East under circumstances which influenced the outlook of those sections toward the Orientals. As the wave of Chinese surged beyond California, the effect on the country was wide and various. Each region which encountered the Orientals reacted in its own way. The confrontation upset humanitarians, confused politicians, and altered the existing notions about the Chinese. The call for Chinese hands in the fields and on the railroads of the South handicapped the Democrats in the East and the West in their stand against Negroes and other colored people. With Chinese strikebreakers threatening the domestic tranquillity of the East, Radical Republicans re-examined their views of racial equality. Northern workingmen, who had shown little concern about Negro slaves in the South, quickly revised their opinions with the arrival of the Chinese in their midst. The spectacle of Southern planters arguing against the importation of Chinese field hands, of Northern industrialists condemning the use of Chinese strikebreakers, of spokesmen of the freedmen favoring the sojourners, and of editors of labor papers hailing the newcomers' arrival revealed the infinite possibilities of the question as a political issue.

A vociferous debate among Americans accompanied the eastward movement. To the sojourners it mattered little whether they accumulated their savings as gold miners in California, field hands in Louisiana, or shoemakers in Massachusetts. Nor did it distress their merchant-creditors as long as the laborers earned the money to pay back the indenture. Nevertheless, both groups preferred California. For the former, it spelled home through the presence of friends, the comforts of Chinatown, and the proximity of their native land. The latter increasingly resisted sending labor companies into the industrial East where their presence created foci for hostile sentiment.

In the 1850's the gold rushes in Oregon and British Columbia were a prelude to the expansion of the mining frontier into the Rocky Mountains. The new discoveries began an intensified Chinese contact with the entire country. The vast extension of the regimented world was also the beginning of the system's decline. Although the control machinery followed the sojourners to their new destinations, their separation from the basis of Chinese life in the United States increased their dependence on the American world for supplies, diversion, and work.

With the movement of the Chinese into the Rocky Mountains and their arrival in the South and East, they made contact with unfamiliar groups of Americans. Metropolitan centers attracted individual Chinese who realized that the United States furnished ways of existence outside the confines of work camp and Chinatown. The discovery contributed to a modification of the sojourners' traditional goal; some began to accept a life in the United States as permanent and gave up the struggle to return to China. The altered outlook closed one era and opened another during which the stranded sojourners became immigrants.

Some Chinese had earlier made contact with the Pacific Northwest. In 1788 fifty Cantonese formed part of Captain John Meares's fur trading post on Nootka Sound. The discovery of gold in the Rogue River country and the establishment of regular steamer connections between San Francisco and Portland in 1851 drew the Chinese vanguard into Oregon Territory.

In the spring of 1858 a "Chinese ambassador" returning from the Fraser River informed the heads of the Five Companies in San Francisco and also the general public about conditions in the mining region. His report described a rich country with miners taking gold out "by the bucketful." Inflamed by these statements, "numbers of Chinese pressed forward with the throngs that shook the wharves of San Francisco in June and July." However, the abandoned claims left behind in the Mother Lode by white miners rushing North opened new opportunities for Chinese mining companies within their established realm in California and kept small the actual number of departing Chinese. Merchants again played the leading role in the migration. In 1864, in behalf of their countrymen, they greeted a newly arriving British governor with "Us be here from year 1858." In answer to the administrator's query, Lee Chang of Kwong Lee & Co. stated that about two thousand Chinese lived on Vancouver Island and in British Columbia, of whom the vast majority engaged in mining.

The work of a ditch company attracted the first large group of Chinese to Nevada Territory in the summer of 1855. Fifty sojourners crossed the mountains and dug a thirty-mile trench to divert the water of the Carson River to the placers in Gold Cañon. At the end of the decade the silver rush to the Nevada mines brought a stream of Chinese wood hawkers, laborers, cooks, and laundrymen to Washoe.

The construction of the Transcontinental Railroad speeded the eastward movement of Chinese into regions theretofore untouched. The feats of docile Chinese construction crews became legendary. Long before guests, journalists, and officers of the Twenty-first Regiment accorded James H. Strowbridge's Chinese foreman three rousing cheers as a public tribute to the construction companies during the ceremony at Promontory Point, some Southern planters had perceived the possibility of using these workers to solve their labor problems.

Labor difficulties had earlier prompted William C. Kelly to bring the only group of Chinese into the ante-bellum South. One of the inventors of the Bessemer iron refining process, Kelly objected to working Christian Negroes as slaves in Kentucky where few whites were willing to do the low labor of an iron factory. Born and raised in Pittsburgh, he had absorbed antislavery sentiment before coming to Eddyville where it was also bad business to contract laborers from slaveholders who required compensation for hired Negroes if they escaped North across the nearby Ohio River. In 1854 Kelly obtained ten Chinese through a New York or Philadelphia tea house to take the place of Blacks at the Suwanee Furnace and Union Forge in Lyon County.

The question of introducing "Chinese labour on our plantations in the place of Negro labour," which had become "hopelessly unmanageable, . . . interested us all very much," Frances Butler Leigh recorded in her journal in 1869. There "seemed to be a general move in this direction all through the Southern states," the lady planter observed. Not being willing to see half her property "uncultivated and going to ruin for want of labor," she, together with her neighbors, agreed "to try the experiment" on her rice plantation near Savannah. During his visit in South Carolina, "Mr. Joseph," a Chinese labor importer from San Francisco, "received letters . . . from . . . planters . . . anxious to make arrangements to secure Chinese labor before the planting season commences," the Charleston *News* reported. "Let the Chinamen come," a series of editorials in the New Orleans *Picayune* urged the deep South, and the letters of the paper's special correspondent from California assured the readers that the Chinese "will be a success on the Southern plantation."

American and Chinese agents arranged the importation of Chinese into the South. The contract agency which facilitated the sojourners' expansion beyond the boundaries of California had appeared during the Chinese advance into the Rocky Mountains. The headmen of the district companies in San Francisco and the storekeepers in the mountain camps had handled the distribution of Chinese mining companies throughout the claims in the Mother Lode. The increased use of Chinese laborers in construction work and the building of the Transcontinental Railroad required the presence of Chinese companies at set dates in work camps along the surveyed route. The race to complete the road put a premium on reliable and punctual labor and created a set of American and Chinese agents. They contracted Chinese workers in San Francisco for specific tasks, or shipped them directly from Hong Kong to wherever their labor was needed. Planters and railroad builders carried the process one step further at the peak of the demand for labor. They sent their own emissaries to California and China to fill their particular needs.

These projects, which aimed at bringing freed Negro plantation workers to terms, also intended to use Chinese in the struggle between capital and labor. The adaptation of the Chinese importation system to labor warfare occasioned the first movement of Chinese sojourners to the East. In three places, North Adams, Massachusetts, Belleville, New Jersey, and Beaver Falls, Pennsylvania, entrepreneurs contracted for Chinese laborers in San Francisco as a weapon against striking American workers.

North Adams had expected the event for days. Finally, on June 13, 1870, two "emigrant cars" rolled into the railroad depot of the small Berkshire hill town. On that Monday, thousands surrounded the station and lined the street leading to Calvin T. Sampson's factory. The strikebreakers had arrived. Seventy-five "pig-tailed, calico-frocked" Chinese debarked and hobbled on wooden shoes to the bunks of their barracks in the rear of a plain, three-story brick structure, the "Model Shoe Factory." When Sampson's frightened mystery weapon in his fight against the Secret Order of the Knights of St. Crispin had finally disappeared behind the well-guarded factory gate, the thirty extra policemen in civilian clothes, the excited spectators, and the pastor of the Congregational Church "were profoundly grateful that the entrance had been effected without bloodshed." The "celestial shoemakers" were a "spectacle which nobody wanted to miss even long enough to stoop for a brickbat." On that Monday night, the Oriental population of Massachusetts more than doubled.

The vanguard of the Chinese stunned the East. Their arrival confused politicians and clergymen, industrialists and labor leaders, editors and poets. "We shall see Sambo and Patrick shaking hands on a common platform— 'Down with the Chinese!,' " the *Alta* predicted from a distance. Northern Democrats also wanted the labor vote but were handicapped by Southern Democrats who speculated on replacing the emancipated slaves in their fields with Chinese laborers. The *Nation,* with apparent delight, recorded the details of the public embarrassment.

Although the people of North Adams accepted the Chinese in their midst, their veiled animosity contrasted with the professional enthusiasm of the reporters of *Harper's* and *Scribner's.* The citizens themselves needed missionaries more than the Chinese, a correspondent of a leading religious weekly concluded after a visit to North Adams. "They've no business here," one woman had told him, "everybody hates 'em but Mr. Sampson, and he worships 'em more than he does his Maker." The Chinese "don't take part in the government," another agreed, "they've no wives or families. They don't mean to stay here. They only come to get money—our money." With the exception of the handful of good Christians who taught the Chinese on Sundays to read and write and the visitors who came to watch the teachers, the people of North Adams saw little of the strangers. The workers made modest purchases in town. On Sundays some wore black American suits, and others entertained their Sunday School teachers at dinner. Only hesitantly did the Chinese leave the confines of their regimented world.

California's attitude toward slavery had shaped the West's encounter with the sojourners. The strange workers in mining and construction companies, governed by the invisible control system of Chinese California, resembled slave gangs and were a constant threat to the California dream. Their regimented world heightened the insecurity of an unstable society that lacked the safety of settled ways on which one of Massachusetts' most northerly manufacturing towns met the newcomers. However, the Crispins' failure to convert the Chinese strikebreakers in North Adams turned Eastern workingmen into determined opponents of Chinese labor and ardent advocates of Chinese exclusion.

The increasing awareness that the United States offered the possibility of living outside their regimented world of work camp and Chinatown encouraged individuals to abandon the control system. The attractions of such metropolitan centers as New York, Philadelphia, Boston, and New Orleans lured sojourners from their familiar path. Together with the impact of the Western world on the bonds of filial piety and familism, the new insights into American life began to modify the sojourners' goal. A small but ever-increasing number of Chinese came to view the United States as a country in which they could live, marry, and raise children. Living in America began to be accepted as a substitute for the traditional aim of returning to China. This change initiated the laborious process which transferred a slowly increasing number of the legion of sojourners into Chinese immigrants.

Until then, their goal had set the Chinese apart from other immigrants and excluded them from the privileges and obligations of newcomers who came to the United States as permanent residents. The sojourners intended to make and save money quickly, and to return to China to a life of ease with the family which their drudgery had maintained. In the clutches of debt bondage or under contract to labor companies, they became docile subjects of bosses and headmen, still directed in the United States by the dictates of the Chinese world, sustained by a control system based on family loyalty and fear. The sojourners shouldered the burden of daily toil in an alien environment in defense of their own system of values. They rejected new standards, and clung to their culture to give meaning to the ordeal.

The sojourners' goal influenced the American reaction. Their world raised up specters that challenged American values. The work camps which regimented anonymous hordes of laborers resembled gangs of Negro slaves. The control system extended debt bondage and despotism to the United States. Chinatown, which harbored indentured emigrants in dilapidated structures, suggested filth and immorality as the sojourners' second nature. These images impressed themselves firmly on Americans and determined the reaction toward the Chinese even after the sojourners had abandoned their traditional goal for the promise of a life defined no longer in terms of mere survival, but of liberty.

V / CONTEMPORARY MIGRATION

Although men had been in motion for millenniums the twentieth century witnessed vaster movements and more complex transfers of population than ever before. Millions continued to stream across the Atlantic from Europe to the Americas, more millions moved to the West as expellees or refugees from eastern Europe, and mass exchanges traded Greeks for Turks and transferred Muslims to Pakistan and Hindus to India. Hundreds of thousands of the remnants of Jewry found refuge in Israel, and hundreds of thousands of Arabs were displaced. In Africa the twentieth century came suddenly upon societies fixed in the mold of earlier times, and independence and urbanization-migration went hand in hand. New patterns of movement took experts to the labor supply instead of labor to the factory centers. In major internal migration Negroes moved militantly northward in the United States. Across hundreds of miles of China Communists made a dramatic march before they established themselves in power. Restrictive legislation was passed in one country after another, but it could barely stem the tide. Countries like Switzerland and Sweden, which had been lands of emigration, became lands of immigration, and population explosion threatened the condition of man. Countries of exodus were both frightened and stimulated by the cultural upheavals accompanying both the departure and the return of the migrant millions.

26 / MASS MIGRATION THEN AND NOW

This comparison of recent migration between different parts of Europe with the earlier mass migration from Europe to the United States relates to many of the significant phenomena of migration: social instability as a cause of migration, the relation between social mobility and migration, the safety-valve theory, migration and the business cycle, the problem of the restriction of emigration and immigration, and so on. The changing conditions of the "market" for immigrants in other continents vitally affect, of course, migration within Europe, and so does the industrial development of countries like France, Western Germany, and Sweden, which have become major countries of immigration.

C. P. Kindleberger, economist, author, former government official, is a professor in Massachusetts Institute of Technology.

The mass migration now taking place from Southern to Northern and Western Europe—from Portugal, Spain, Italy, Greece and Turkey to Switzerland, France, Germany and Belgium—can be measured against the movement from Southern and Eastern Europe to the United States between 1880 and 1913 for similarities and differences. It is particularly instructive to observe whether previous pitfalls have been avoided, and if so, whether by accident, by circumstances or because of the increased social consciousness of the human race.

The economic, social and political importance of the two movements is difficult to overstate. In both cases, cheap labor fed economic growth by holding down wages, relatively at least, and maintaining high rates of profit, investment and expansion. The migrants constituted the "reserve armies of the unemployed" which Marx believed were necessary for capitalism to feed on. The Marxist model is by no means the only road to the growth of income—over-all, but also, be it noted, per head as well. In some situations it is possible for economic growth to be stimulated by mass emigration: clearing up redundant labor, or disguised unemployment, stimulates the economy by increasing the return to efficient utilization of resources, and in particular encourages the adoption of machinery which saves total resources as well as labor. Just as Ireland benefited from emigration in the nineteenth century, so Southern Italy, Spain and Greece enjoy high rates of economic growth today while their citizens contribute to growth in the North.

The evident similarities of the two mass movements go beyond their contribution to growth. Immigration in the United States in the last century was disjointed; Europe's is today. In the United States, the first wave came from England, Germany, Scandinavia and Ireland,

C. P. Kindleberger, "Mass Migrations Then and Now," excerpted by permission from the July 1965 issue of *Foreign Affairs* (vol. 43, #4), 647–658. Copyright by the Council on Foreign Relations, Inc., New York.

reaching a peak in 1882. Thereafter the source shifted to Southern and Eastern Europe—especially Italy, Austria-Hungary and Russia.

*　　*　　*

The first migrants went into agriculture to replace natives who had moved on—out to the frontier in the United States, and into industry or trade in Europe. The succeeding wave went into "dirty jobs": mining, construction and heavy metal work like blast furnaces for men; textiles and domestic service for women. Unskilled work was turned over almost entirely to the immigrant, so much so that all Swiss now hold down skilled or semiskilled jobs.

A final similarity is only now emerging in the fact that the capacity of a country to absorb immigrants is limited, and that after a time it will make efforts to call a halt to inward movement. These limits are reached sooner for immigrants of different races than people of similar stock. The Chinese Exclusion Act of 1882 parallels the de facto restrictions of North Africans and colored races by France and Britain. German employment of Moroccans and South Koreans in mining is an exception explained by the Hallstein doctrine, under which West Germany is especially friendly to countries which refuse to recognize East Germany. After the initial restrictions on Chinese and Japanese in the United States came qualitative restriction—prohibitions against the sick, paupers and, under the Foran Act of 1885, against contract labor. . . .

Some countries of Europe—Britain, Austria, the Netherlands and Scandinavia—do not as a rule admit Southern Europeans, but the country which has the most—Switzerland—is now experiencing a revulsion on social and political grounds which has given rise to executive restriction, a refusal to ratify an agreement with Italy for increased rights for immigrants, and even a petition for a constitutional amendment restricting foreign-born residents to 10 per cent of the native population.

That immigrants are still accorded a warm welcome in Belgium, France and Germany may be attributed to their limited numbers, as compared with those who came to the United States. Here the foreign-born constituted about 20 per cent of the labor force in 1890 and 1900, as compared with 4 per cent in Germany, about 9 per cent in France, 10 per cent in Belgium and 30 per cent in Switzerland currently. . . .

*　　*　　*

Scale, then, is an important difference for all but Switzerland. Another apparent difference is that the migrant to America turned his back on the old world and sought a new life, whereas the European migrant today is a transient, who seeks his fortune abroad for a few years and then plans to return home. Whether he actually does go home, time alone will tell.

But the statement that immigrants to America turned their backs on the old country is not substantiated. Many of the Italians and Greeks who came to the United States were seasonal workers, *golodrinos,* or swallows, who came in the spring and returned as winter approached.

Departures from the United States between 1897 and 1918 were almost half as many as arrivals (47 per cent). The longer they stayed the less was the likelihood of return. Of some two million returning after 1908 who answered a government questionnaire, 77 per cent had been in the United States less than five years.

But if more returned from the United States than is generally believed, the opposite is true in Europe. It is still too early after 1961 to know what proportions will stay abroad, but early postwar experience as investigated in studies sponsored by UNESCO makes clear what the answer depends on. Young men who come abroad will return—unless they marry a local girl. Older men or those already married will return—unless they bring their wives and stay long enough for their children to go to the local school, form friendships with the natives and push roots into the local soil. Major conditioning factors are whether they live in a ghetto or intermingle with local populace, how quickly they learn the native language, how frequently they return home on leave.

This open question is fraught with considerable significance for Europe. France wants the immigrants to settle permanently and fill the demographic void left by the low birth rates prior to 1946 and the war losses. Greece, on the other hand, is fearful that her national existence is threatened by the effusion of her best people—since foreign employers take mainly the healthy, the young, the politically innocent and the skilled. Italy favors freedom of individual choice. Germany has not yet begun to think about the long-run impact. Spain is fearful that returning workers who have breathed freedom beyond the Pyrenees will find the domestic political air suffocating.

Moreover, the Swiss have found that the economic benefits of immigration change with time and permanent settlement. In the short run, with excess capacity of plant but full employment of labor, immigration pays off. Wages are held down, profits are maintained; it is the best of all possible economic worlds. In time, however, high profits stimulate plant expansion, which makes it not only desirable, but now imperative to have foreign workers. And as the foreign workers stay on they require capital expansion for themselves: housing, schools, hospitals. One in every fifth child born in Switzerland today has foreigners as parents; in Zurich hospital corridors and wards on Sunday afternoons, it is said, one can hear mainly Italian spoken, and with more animation than Swiss sobriety considers seemly. Foreign funds in Switzerland are no longer held liquid or reinvested abroad, but are increasingly needed to construct industrial and social capital to go with the foreign workers. With foreign capital and foreign labor, the Swiss are supplying only the real estate and the management, and feel themselves in a precarious position. They are economically damned if the foreign workers leave, and politically and socially altered beyond all recognition if they stay. But as each year goes by, the chances of their staying increase.

There may then be a difference in the permanence of immigration, but it is too early to be certain. Other differences are surely present. In the United States, the foreign worker was used as a strikebreaker. In Europe, if he comes in at all, the unions welcome him. It is true that labor unions in Britain, Holland and the Scandinavian countries account in large part for the policy of exclusion followed by these countries. In Sweden, it has gone so far that the government has yielded sovereignty on the question to the unions. Employer requests for foreign workers are referred by the government to the union, and if the latter objects, the request is refused. . . .

Not only are the foreign workers not strikebreakers in Europe today; they may be the strike makers. The strike in the Asturias coal mines was supported by contributions from Spanish miners in the Ruhr. Foreign workers drop their tools when unions call strikes. Where the workers are admitted, solidarity reigns. But the difference must not be exaggerated. Immigrants were strikebreakers in the United States only through ignorance. Strenuous efforts were made to keep the involuntary scabs from contact with the regular workers. Where this screen was penetrated, the foreign workers left the plant too, on numerous occasions. And in Europe today it is very hard to get the southern worker with his weak union tradition to pay high dues, attend meetings or participate in routine union life. . . .

*   *   *

The major difference between nineteenth-century America and twentieth-century Europe lies in the correction, or at least the attempt at correction, of the abuses of exploitation which such mass movements can lead to. In Germany and France, for example, the recruiting is done by government as well as by employer. The contract system so vehemently denounced in the United States and prohibited in 1885 is the established means of operation, run by the governments of both countries in collaboration. Runners, padrones and boss interpreters lurk at the fringes of the system, but are systematically repressed. There is a substantial private movement of workers from Italy into Germany and France as tourists. Under the regulations of the European Economic Community, citizens of one country have rights to work almost equal to those of natives. Portuguese padrones smuggle peasants into France, jammed into ships and moving clandestinely at night, but this survives only because of ignorance, since a governmental agreement in 1964 made the movement legal. Some Germans object that the foreign worker with a one-year contract has more protection than the native-born employee who is without a contract. This applies only to the last in. Those who have worked for more than a year are on an equal footing. It is evident that no country in Europe will dare to force the weight of recession exclusively on the foreign worker; international public opinion will not allow a country to repeat the French action of the 1930s in canceling the visas of Poles and Italians, loading them on trains and shipping them home.

The recruitment and allocation of workers have thus been taken into government hands for the most part. Working conditions are supervised. Living varies from country to country. Company towns exist in many places, especially in Germany, where many of the larger companies, but not all, have constructed barracks for single workers. These are typically organized along national lines with a kitchen to enable the foreign workers to cook their native fare. In France, however, and to a lesser degree in Switzerland, housing conditions more closely resemble the notorious boardinghouses, usually run by a compatriot, which provide minimal comfort and nutrition at substantial prices. Last summer the French authorities closed down a so-called "merchant of sleep" in Lyon who had 50 beds, occupied three times daily, in a normal house. Equally insalubrious are the so-called Paris hotels where congregate the African migrants from the *Communauté* largely from a single migrant tribe, the Saraholes, whose land lies in Senegal, Mali and Mauritania.

Housing is a serious problem from any points of view. It is short for the native population throughout Europe. The foreign worker with a family at home is anxious to spend as little abroad as he can. To require him to have comfortable housing and to pay its market value is to force him to accumulate capital at a slower rate than he wants, against his return when he wants to buy a farm or a business, or pay off old debts. He seeks overtime work, hangs around the station on the weekend to avoid spending money at the café, and crowds together in inexpensive barracks to save. Swiss citizens are disturbed at the rash of signs for rented rooms, saying "No foreigners need apply," but the landlord's defense is a legitimate one: a room rented to one Italian often is used by ten, with serious consequences for the property in dilapidation. Compare John R. Commons' remark in "Races and Immigrants in America" that the competition of races is the competition of standards of living: "The reason the Chinaman or the Italian can save three days' wages is because wages have been previously fixed by the greater necessities of the more advanced races." . . .

The enlarged role of the state is not to make up for lack of private interest. The benevolent societies organized on religious and national lines in the United States in the nineteenth century are matched in Europe today. *Caritas,* the Catholic welfare agency in Germany, provides meeting places, like settlement houses, for the workers from Portugal, Spain and Italy. Lacking immigrants from a Protestant country, the Evangelical Church has underwritten the welfare work among the Orthodox Greeks. The Moslem Turks had no religious group to look out for them, a vacuum which the agnostic trade-union movement undertook to fill. Germany today has three mosques for Moslem worship, one in Frankfurt, one in Cologne and one mounted on a flatcar with a tower which folds down for passage under bridges and through tunnels, which accompanies the large railroad construction crews from Turkey.

Here, then, is a wide difference: the enormous movement of population is not left to laissez-faire but attracts the efforts of government at all stages. In the United States, the states regulated abuses (as early as 1847 in New York), but the Federal Government operated only to slow down the movement and ultimately to turn it off. In Europe it is under continuous government surveillance and control. . . .

There is one more difference in which the United States does not come off too badly: citizenship. When a man did stay five years, and learned the language, he was eligible to become an American citizen and to vote on a par with the native born. This was the expectation. In Europe it is the exception.

It is possible for a foreign immigrant to become a citizen in Europe, but difficult. What Italians and Spanish in Switzerland focus on is not citizenship but the right to stay permanently, won after only three years' residence, although the proposed treaty with Italy would reduce the time to 18 months. The Algerians, and members of the *Communauté* who have citizenship, have lost the free right of entry, but the members of the Common Market who have free right of entry have no easy road to citizenship. This waits on economic integration going so far that it leads to social and ultimately political integration.

This is the European dilemma, which time must resolve. If the Mediterranean immigrants stay in the North and West for economic reasons, they must have social and political equality. If they go home, the question is what will become of them.

The agricultural worker from, say, Norway, who went into farming in America and later returned, was a changed man—experimental, innovating, discontented with the routine methods in his native land. But the Italian peasant who went into industry in the United States found it hard to fit in when he came home. He had money which he loaned out rather than invested in a new business of his own; but he had acquired no agricultural and few industrial skills. America had changed his clothes and his appearance, but his goals remained what they had been when he left—to get off the farm and into the city. Many Turks returning from Germany these days bring back large American second-hand cars and set themselves up in *dolmus* businesses —half-taxi, half-bus—in Ankara or Istanbul. Some Italian firms have recruited back Italian workers in German cities, giving us the curious phenomenon that Germany, recruiting workers in Southern Italy and losing them to Northern, is providing mobility to the Italian labor force which the country had difficulty in achieving for itself. But even if they go back to their own country, it is not clear that they can readily be absorbed.

This, then, is the danger—that the mass migrant of today will become a man without a country, one who has left one life and finds that he cannot stay where he is and cannot go home again. The problem of belonging is difficult enough within one's own borders. Unless Europe achieves a social and political identity, it may develop a problem of "flying Mediterraneans," restless spirits with no home.

27 / REFUGEE MIGRATION IN THE TWENTIETH CENTURY

The world has known refugees for thousands of years, but the increase of population and of national consciousness and the wider coordination of wars have intensified the problem in the twentieth century. Although refugees may be considered the most unfortunate of all migrants, it should be recognized that often the only alternatives facing large communities are annihilation and refugee-migration. These enormous transfers of peoples have been made possible by a variety of new factors—improved public health measures, advances in the techniques and means of transportation, and, perhaps most vital of all, a quickened sense of social responsibility, the concept that we are "our brother's keeper." By the intensive work of both private and inter-governmental refugee agencies millions of lives have been spared in our time, lives which in earlier epochs would have been snuffed out in mass slaughter or starvation. Here are both a general view and a few specific examples of the modern refugee problem from the pen of Professor Louise Holborn, a scholar who has been active in this field for many years, and who is now professor of government in the Radcliffe Institute for Independent Study, Cambridge, Massachusetts.

Modern refugee movements, beginning in Europe and subsequently becoming world-wide, have given rise to a new class of people who are homeless and stateless and who live in a condition of constant insecurity which erodes human dignity. They have caused grave political and economic problems for the countries of temporary reception, problems which have proved too burdensome for the administrative facilities and financial resources of private organizations and national governments. The refugee problem has thus transcended national jurisdiction and institutions.

Furthermore, while in its earlier stages the refugee problem was seen as a temporary and limited phenomenon, it has now come to be acknowledged as universal, continuing, and recurring. In response to this challenge the international community has developed a complex mechanism of world-wide cooperation involving a tripartite partner-

Louise Holborn, "The World Refugee Problem," excerpted with the permission of the publisher from the *International Encyclopedia of the Social Sciences*, David L. Sills, ed., Vol. XIII, pp. 361–373. Copyright © 1968 by Crowell Collier and Macmillan, Inc.

ship of national governments, private agencies, and international organizations; no longer confined by strict definitions of the word "refugee," it is prepared to approach the problem in all its various aspects—political, social, economic, and humanitarian.

• • •

Europe in the twentieth century has been a vast arena of refugee movements set in motion by the disruptions of war, the breakup of empires, the impact of violent nationalism, and the arbitrary actions of dictatorial regimes. Early in the century political turbulence in the Balkans and Asia Minor resulted in the movement of hundreds of thousands of people from one country to another, culminating in large exchanges of populations, in particular of Greeks, Bulgars, Serbs, Armenians, and Turks. The Convention of Lausanne, January 30, 1923, stipulated a compulsory exchange of populations between Greece and Turkey. A total of 1.3 million Greeks, including tens of thousands from Russia and Bulgaria, were transferred to Greece, and about 400,000 Turks to Turkey. The Convention of Neuilly, November 27, 1919, provided for a voluntary exchange of populations between Greece and Bulgaria, and between 1913 and 1925 more than 220,000 Bulgars moved into the truncated territories of Bulgaria. After the Russian collapse in 1917, 30,000 Assyrians who had fought against the Turks escaped to the Caucasus, Greece, and Iraq and later to Syria. Armenians fled from persecution and massacre in Asia Minor following the collapse of the Ottoman Empire and the rise of Turkish nationalism. By 1923 an estimated 320,000 Armenian refugees were scattered in the Middle East, the Balkans, and other European countries.

About 1.5 million Russian nationals were dispersed and left stranded in north, central, and southern Europe and in the Far East as a result of the Bolshevik Revolution of November 1917, the rout of the anti-Bolshevik armies in European Russia in 1919–1920, the famine of 1921, and the collapse of White Russian resistance in Siberian Russia in 1922.

The ranks of refugees were further increased by those in flight from dictatorships in Spain, Germany, and Italy. Some 140,000 of the Spanish refugees who sought refuge in France between 1937 and 1939 remained in that country after the Spanish Civil War came to an end; smaller numbers, especially children, were evacuated to Great Britain, Belgium, Mexico, and the Soviet Union; between 40,000 and 50,000 fled to North Africa. Between 1933 and the outbreak of World War

II, more than a million refugees—political, religious, and racial (most of them Jews)—left Germany; many succeeded in fleeing to Western Europe or across the seas, but nearly 700,000 of them remained in the territories subsequently occupied by Germany and its allies. Refugees from Italian dictatorship numbered 65,000 to 70,000 in 1938; many of them went to North Africa.

Refugees in World War II

World War II cause the most formidable displacement of population ever experienced. First, there was the mass movement of Germans within Greater Germany. Ethnic Germans were transferred into Germany, mainly from Eastern Europe; it has been estimated that approximately 600,000 persons had been transferred into the German Reich by spring 1942. Other government measures for the movement of German nationals included the dispersal of industry in Germany, the colonization of the conquered territories, and evacuation from bomb-target urban centers. In addition, hundreds of thousands of German Jews were herded into concentration and extermination camps. Finally, large numbers of Germans fled from the path of the victorious Allied armies. Then there was the displacement of non-Germans: those expelled from the defeated countries; those whose movement was effected by agreements or treaties for the transfer and exchange of populations; those dispatched to 'Greater Germany' as prisoners of war or forced laborers; and those non-Germans, mostly Jews, systematically deported from the defeated countries to the concentration camps of Germany. It has been estimated that by May 1945 there were 40.5 million uprooted people in Europe, excluding non-German forced laborers and those Germans who fled before the advancing Soviet armies.

Post-War Refugees from Eastern Europe

As a result of the Communist coup in Czechoslovakia in February 1948, 60,000 Czech refugees fled to the western zones of Germany and of Austria. At the outbreak of the Hungarian Revolution in October 1956, more than 200,000 Hungarian refugees poured over the borders into Austria (180,000) and Yugoslavia (20,000). There is still a small but steady flow of escapees from the Communist countries of Eastern Europe, estimated at the end of 1964, to be between 12,000 and 15,000 per year. (A similar number are escaping from Communist China to other Asian countries.)

"Repatriates" to European Countries

The 9.5 million German "expellees" from the territories east of the Oder-Neisse River, the 3.3 million persons from Eastern and Southern Europe, and the nearly 65,000 persons who moved, under governmental agreement for family reunion, from East to West, were national and ethnic German refugees for whom the West German Government assumed responsibility. Similar problems attended the liquidation of European colonial regimes. For instance, the years 1945–1958 saw the repatriation of many French citizens from former French territories in Asia and Africa; 75,000 returned from Indo-China after the establishment of independent Vietnam, 10,000 left both before and after the establishment of the Republic of Guinea in 1958; 138,000 came from Tunisia and 172,000 from Morocco after the attainment of independence by these countries in 1956. More than 15,000 French citizens left Egypt after the Suez Crisis in 1956, and some 950,000 more left Algeria during and after the struggle for independence which culminated in the establishment of an independent republic in 1962. The Netherlands received about 300,000 Dutch Indonesians, when Indonesia became an independent state in 1949.

All the above were accepted by their respective countries as national refugees, i.e. as legal citizens. The relationship between the repatriates and the indigenous population was very strained at first, particularly in regard to employment and social adjustment; but their national governments assisted in the settlement and integration of the newcomers and, in the case of the Dutch-Indonesian, in the resettlement of many overseas.

Refugees in Asia

In the second half of the twentieth century the scene of mass population movements has shifted away from Europe to Asia. The people involved have tended to come from a simple agricultural setting and their flight, for the most part, has been to equally undeveloped and often politically unstable countries. The result has been widespread destitution and misery.

Vietnam

Mass refugee movements occurred during and after the Armistice Conference held in Geneva in July 1954 which terminated hostilities in Vietnam, Laos, and Cambodia. Art. 1 of the Convention provided for the division of Vietnam at the 17th parallel (a "provisional military demarcation line"): the Viet-Minh (People's Army of Viet-Nam) were to the North and the French Union forces to the South. Civilians were to be allowed to move freely from one zone to the other, and the authorities of each zone were to assist their movement. By May 18, 1955, the final evacuation date, 860,000 persons (of whom 676,000 were Catholics) had left North Vietnam for South Vietnam. In addition to Vietnamese, about 42,000 semi-nomadic tribesmen joined the flight to the south. Because of communication problems and the opposition of Viet-Minh forces, their flight was a difficult and dangerous undertaking. French military and civilian planes flew many refugees south and the U. S. Navy task force transported others by sea from embarkation points along the coast. Two Vietnamese organizations, the Refugee Commission and the Catholic Committee on Resettlement of Refugees, were aided by the governments of the United States, France, Philippines, New Zealand, and Australia, and also by UNICEF, WHO, and various private charitable organizations. By 1960, 315 refugee villages had been established by the newcomers on undeveloped agricultural land and, in the normal course, the integration of the refugees would soon have been completed.

However, in face of gradually intensifying military and guerilla activities in the South since 1954, large numbers of refugees have moved from unsafe areas in search of shelter and protection. These later movements have occurred for a variety of reasons: panic flight from areas of military operation; escape from Vietcong terrorism, extortion, and recruitment; and movement away from Communist-controlled areas, both at the urging of religious leaders, and as a result of government resettlement programs. In addition, some have left their homes because of typhoons and floods. By January 31, 1966, the Agency for International Development (AID) reported an estimated 1 million refugees in South Vietnam.

The Government of South Vietnam, with the assistance of AID and 24 American voluntary agencies, has developed an ambitious program of assistance for emergency and long-range services, including programs that attempt to increase the refugees' productivity in resettlement areas. It is hoped that as many of the refugees as possible will eventually return to their villages in peace.

Palestine Arab Refugees

The UN decision to partition Palestine was followed by the 1948–49 Arab-Israel conflict and the flight of an estimated 500,000 people from their homes in the area of fighting. Of these, the majority were Arabs, with a smattering of Armenians, Greeks, and non-Jewish nationals of other countries. By June 30, 1966, 1,317,000 were registered with the United Nations Relief and Works Agency for Palestine Refugees in the Near East (UNRWA): 707,000 in Jordan, 307,000 in the Gaza strip, 164,000 in Lebanon, and 140,000 in Syria (UNRWA). From the outset, the compilation of accurate statistics on the refugees was made extremely difficult; for political reasons, and out of a desire for additional material aid, figures were inflated by false registrations and unreported deaths. UNRWA was established by the UN in 1949 as a temporary organization. But since substantial progress in the reintegration of the refugees, either by repatriation or by resettlement has not materialized, the mandate of the agency has several times been extended. With the cooperation of the Arab host governments and international organizations, UNRWA attempts the dual task of providing relief and assisting refugees to become productive and self-supporting.

By June 30, 1965, 70 per cent of the refugees received basic dry rations, and 40 per cent had been sheltered in 54 camps, the rest having found their own accommodation. More than 228,000 children were going to school, 168,000 of them in the 406 UNRWA-UNESCO schools. UNRWA operates 10 vocational or teachers training centers and undertakes basic preventive and curative health care through 88 clinics and other facilities; in addition, more than 250,000 refugees, mainly children, benefit from UNRWA's programs of supplementary feeding and milk distribution. From May 1, 1950 to December 31, 1965, UNRWA spent close to $535 million, contributed to a large extent by the U.S.

However, the problem of the Palestine Arab refugees is as much political as socio-economic. Until a political solution is achieved, these refugees will continue as a symbol and focus of instability and unrest in the Middle East.

Israel

The persecution of the Jews by Nazi Germany was an important factor in speeding up the establishment of the Jewish national home first envisaged in the Balfour Declaration of 1917. Immigration of Jews into Palestine, which had continued both openly and clandestinely since the end of World War I, became legally unrestricted upon the establishment of the state of Israel in 1948. An ambitious resettlement program has been pursued by the government of Israel, involving a total of 1,209,282 immigrants by 1964, the majority being refugees from the countries of Central and Eastern Europe, North Africa, and the Middle East. The Jewish Agency for Israel, the Joint Distribution Committee, and the United Jewish Appeal, as well as the intergovernmental Committee for European Migration and the United Nations High Commissioner for Refugees have assisted in this work.

28 / ISRAELI MELTING POT

One of the most dramatic—at once disturbing and constructive— of all the examples of twentieth-century migration was the vast re-migration of Jews to Palestine. Those fervent devotees of a national and religious ideal have made the desert to bloom and the machines to whir, but by their very success they have enhanced the resentment of their Arab neighbors.

In 1882 only some 24,000 Jews lived in their ancient ancestral land. Gradual resettlement brought the figure to 85,000 in 1914, then war and privation reduced it to 56,000 in 1918. Under the British mandate the Jews came to number 650,000 by 1948, with 90 per cent of the immigration coming from Europe. Under independence the Law of the Return promised any Jew from anywhere the right to live in Israel. A million and a quarter poured in within the next twenty years, 55 per cent of them from Asian and African backgrounds in stark contrast with the cultural heritage of their predecessors. From Iraq alone came 120,000, and many countries simply sent their entire Jewish population to Israel. Except for religion they thought and lived more like the surrounding Arabs. Nevertheless, in 1966 the population was composed of 2,600,000 Jews and only about 300,000 non-Jews. The war of 1967 resulted in the addition, at least temporarily, of 1,100,000 Arabs.

Most significant for the future was the fact that the European-American Jewish immigration had been largely in the older age brackets; the Asian and African immigration was of families in lower age brackets and with a much larger birth rate.

Hal Lehrman, an experienced correspondent, caught the spirit of this immigrant surge at its peak and saw at first hand the complex cultural problems created by the sudden and uniquely diverse influx of Jews from all points of the compass.

From Hal Lehrman, *Israel, The Beginning and Tomorrow.* New York: William Sloane Associates, 1948. Pages 57–67. Reprinted by permission of William Morrow and Company, Inc. Copyright © 1951 by Hal Lehrman.

The task of westernizing the young state in spirit as well as intention would have been difficult enough if the builders of Israel had been confronted only by the 650,000 Jews present in Palestine at the moment of Israel's birth. But modernization was made almost intolerably complicated by a policy of "unlimited" immigration which doubled the population in three years. That policy flooded a land and a society not equipped to receive them with masses of variegated, totally dissimilar newcomers from all corners of the world—and predominantly from the more underprivileged corners.

During the mandate, the rate of immigration had averaged 18,000 per year; the independent state expanded it to an average of nearly 18,000 per month, and in some months the figure reached 30,000, or 1,000 per day. Nothing like it had been witnessed in modern times. The "Open Door" program was magnificently daring—a policy from which older, greater, vastly more richly endowed countries would have recoiled in dismay. But it also imposed colossal problems of physical maintenance, economic stability and human relations.

Emotionally, the policy was dictated by the most compelling of Zionist tenets reaching back into millennial tradition and Biblical promise. It could be found in Isaiah, when God had pledged "I will bring thy seed from the East and gather thee from the West; I will say to the North, give up, and to the South, keep not back: bring my sons from far, and my daughters from the ends of the earth. . . ." In the Israel Proclamation of Independence it was declared unequivocally that the state "will be open to the immigration of Jews from all countries of their dispersion." For Zionism, Israel was an instrument rather than a goal, the supreme end and purpose of statehood being to provide a homeland for all who wished to forsake the Diaspora and to "return." Accordingly, as its first act after independence and as a token of Israel's whole dedication to *Kibbutz Galuyot* (The Ingathering of the Exiles), the provisional government rendered nil the 1939 British White Paper, which had curtailed Jewish immigration and land acquisition. And by unanimous vote on July 5, 1950, the Israel parliament passed the "Law of the Return," where it was solemnly proclaimed that "every Jew has the right to immigrate to Israel."

There was another reason, no less imperative in the judgment of the regime, for the speedy influx: an urgent need for population. Population to deepen the manpower reservoir whence the tiny state might draw its fighters in event of renewed assault from the hostile and numerically overwhelming Arab territories which hemmed it in on all sides except the sea. Population to cover the expanse of the land, fill up the vulnerable empty spaces, garrison the new interior settlements and the fortress-colonies girdling the exposed frontiers. Population to work the farms and the factories required for the enlarged and modernized economy which Israel must develop to achieve and hold a westernized standard of living.

Naturally, this self-interested motive for large immigration received less public emphasis than the more altruistic theme of rescuing the exiles, since the former stressed a potential contribution of the newcomers *to* the state rather than the exalted mission of refuge and shelter. But the practical advantages of the ingathering, from the point of view of military and economic planning, were nonetheless prominent in the considerations of the Israel leaders, and offset to their satisfaction the great risks of the unprecedented population increase.

Thus, idealism and strategy combined to justify the bold policy of record-shattering immigration. The policy was all the more implementable because of the very real pressures from substantial segments of dispersed communities clamoring to migrate. Each crisis of "repatriation" was liquidated only to be replaced by a fresh one. The DP camps of Germany and Austria and Italy were emptied; but then the gates of oppressed Yemen opened; and then a "deadline" for Polish emigration had to be met; and suddenly the government of Rumania decided to permit mass departures, so Jewry had to be transported as rapidly as possible from there before Bucharest changed its mind and shut the doors once more; and meanwhile the situation in Iraq spilled over into a crisis. So it went, each dramatic demand on Israel's hospitality keeping at white heat the fervor for *Kibbutz Galuyot,* marshaling public opinion inside Israel to renewed sacrifice and public opinion among world Jewry to renewed financial aid—and incidentally facilitating the government's basic program for a larger Israel people.

Strictly speaking, the immigration was not entirely "unlimited." Where feasible, persons with communicable diseases or otherwise incapacitated were given prolonged treatment prior to entry into Israel. With funds inadequate for all areas at once, priorities were established for certain areas, such as Rumania and Iraq. Delays were encouraged elsewhere: In North Africa particularly, pre-training and rehabilitation before emigration were emphasized, propaganda in favor of exodus was restrained, the quota of visas was reduced. But such devices were controls rather than limitations: in terms of volume and dimension, the immigration was so large—so clearly vaster than reception facilities —that it could scarcely be described as anything but free and unfettered.

The result of this immigration policy was a complex of staggering problems so difficult of solution that many sympathetic observers, both at home and abroad, questioned the wisdom of incurring obligations of such magnitude in addition to the normal but already grievous burdens of pioneer statehood.

Apart from the immense cost of transportation, reception and preliminary integration—an expense largely defrayed by foreign philanthropy—there was first of all the desperate need to find physical facilities for the hundreds of thousands of newcomers, to provide them with temporary shelter and then permanent housing, to create opportunities for employment, to develop the public works projects, the agricultural settlements and the new or expanded industries which might supply the wages, grow the food, produce the goods essential for the absorption, self-support and plain survival of the immigrant masses.

The first wave of newcomers was handled with relative dispatch, thanks to the availability of abandoned Arab towns and villages which were more or less repaired and adapted for immigrant occupation. Nearly 200,000 *olim* (immigrants) were accommodated under tolerable conditions in this way. But as the Arab areas filled up, the period of waiting in the initial transient camps lengthened. At one moment, eventually, over 100,000 persons—about 10 per cent of the country's entire population—were living in these primitive reception centers. Men, women and children crowded indiscriminately into huts and tents amid abysmal sanitation and general squalor. Despite monumental efforts by the government, the Jewish Agency and auxiliary organizations, the turnover was very slow, forcing months of aimless, nonproductive and morale-draining existence on the immigrants before their removal to more acceptable quarters and an opportunity for self-sustaining labor. These conditions were somewhat relieved after a time by the inauguration of transit work villages (*ma'abarot*), to which immigrants were transferred without protracted delay and where they could find partial employment and some degree of community living. But there too the standards of hygiene and housing were wretchedly low, and life remained essentially a matter of waiting again for still another transfer.

Meanwhile the construction of permanent housing lagged—for lack of funds and basic materials—far behind building schedules and the sheer need. Types of homes ranged from cement dwellings to imported prefabs of Austrian, Finnish or Swedish design and corrugated tin huts. Space was restricted to minimum requirements: a family of four was entitled to one room plus a small alcove for washing, cooking and storage. Even so, permanent construction was utterly unable to keep pace with immigration. The rate of annual building, three years after creation of the state, produced scarcely half of the structures which would have been required to house just the immigrants who arrived that same year.

• • •

Less apparent than the material shortages in immigrant absorption, but at least as important for the long-term stability of the state, were the intricate problems of immigrant civic, social and cultural assimilation in the new society.

The post-independence *aliyah* (immigration) differed unfavorably in numerous crucial aspects from the various cycles of immigration which had previously fertilized the ethnic soil of Jewish Palestine. Gone was the pioneering élan of the *halutzim,* trained in or inspired by the Zionist ideal, eager to pit their fervor and physical vigor against the desert and make it yield fruit.

The newcomers into Israel underwent little scrutiny or screening. The aged and the infirm, the weary and the disillusioned all poured in alike, seeking not adventure but peace—and feeling in the main, many even belligerently, that they had a right to it. Those Europeans who had survived war, the concentration camps and the Nazi crematoria had little stomach for the rugged living of pioneer camp settlements. Those who had shaken the dust of Communist-ruled Eastern Europe from their running feet were not burning to embrace the collectivist philosophies of Israel's communal colonies. As for the Oriental masses, they were generally not even aware of the meaning of colonization, a concept quite absent from their semi-medieval intellectual baggage. For them Israel was the land of the Bible, not of Theodor Herzl.

One of the first casualties of the new era, therefore, was the kibbutz, the cooperative rural community which had been the great hope and one of the most original contributions of pre-Israel Palestine. Already internally shaken by the same East-West political differences which were tormenting socialist institutions everywhere in the postwar world, the kibbutzim of Israel had begun to grow progressively less vital to the economy and social structure of the state as the population increased: the colonies were failing to attract the recruits needed to maintain even their proportionate prominence in the expanding country. Unless the ideal could somehow be reanimated and adapted to the changing hour, the kibbutz of early glory might in another generation dwindle into little better than a vestigial growth on the body of the new Zion.

Gone as well from the current onrush of population was the economic resourcefulness, the wealth, machinery and techniques which had marked the German Jewish emigration of the Hitler period. With exceptions not sufficiently frequent for real effect, the present arrivals came empty of hand, possessing little or no funds to finance a fresh start. Only a relatively few from the DP camps had employed their spare time and talents to acquire a nest egg for Israel operations. The Yugoslavs and Bulgarians who departed almost en masse for Israel had, on the whole, only a trace of their pre-war material goods; the Poles, the Rumanians and the rare Hungarians who were allowed to leave were compelled to abandon nearly everything. The bulk of the self-exiles from Turkey and North Africa were the most impoverished elements of those communities; those who were not already penniless before they registered for exodus from Iraq were despoiled on the eve of their departure by the freezing of bank deposits, large-scale confiscation of property, and even the rifling (by "customs inspectors") of the miserable bundles of personal clothing and family keepsakes packed for travel. The Yemenites, almost to a man, had little of value to bring to Israel except their water-pipes, their rugs and their sacred books.

Some of the DP's from Europe, after the years of Nazi death-camp debasement in the dog-eat-dog fight for survival, had themselves grown hard and brutal; others emerged apathetic, bewildered, divested of initiative, incapable of revitalization without long and patient care. Barely 1 per cent of the total immigration in the first three years of Israel's existence had a profession. Better than 50 per cent was entirely unskilled, with no trade or craft at all. Even among those who did possess a skill, many found it impossible under local conditions to follow the occupation at which they had worked in their own countries. The problems of occupational adjustment were well-nigh universal, and in the majority of cases the immigrant began his long and painful road of economic absorption almost from scratch.

Fundamental to the social confusion caused by the undigested immigrant mass was the chaos of national origins. No less than sixty-one nationalities were represented in the influx. These transformed Israel into a "melting pot" which contained such an intense variety in its boiling stew that even the complex pattern during the heyday of immigration into the United States seemed almost simple by comparison.

Jews from Budapest shared tents with Jews from Hadhramaut Arabia. Kurds and Afghans mingled, in mutual wonder, with Parisians and Viennese. There were Iraqui whose ancestors had been freed by King Cyrus, and Iranians who claimed descent from the exiles to Babylon. Dark, soft-spoken folk from India, others from inner China with traces of the Mongolian strain, walked side by side with ex-merchants and storekeepers from Sofia and Bratislava. Lebanese, Syrians; Balts, Czechs, Greeks, Ukrainians; Yemenites and their kinsmen from the British Crown Colony of Aden; and from North Africa alone three distinct nationalities—Tunisian, Algerian, Moroccan—and four distinct origins: Berber Jews who spoke the *shilhi* dialect, Arabic-speaking Jews from Moslem Spain, Spanish Jews from Christian Spain who spoke Ladino, and immigrants who had come to the southwestern Mediterranean from various points in Europe during the nineteenth and twentieth centuries.

How unify this kaleidoscopic diversity? Variety could generate a rich dynamism when synthetized—yet how distill from this heady elixir not the lowest common essence but a brave new mixture of the finest and the best? Most perplexing of all, in what way evolve from the backward, heterogeneous Oriental masses a Western-minded, assimilable modern man? . . .

The older settlers in Israel generally accepted and even were strongly in favor of the immigration policy, from humane, Zionist and patriotic motivations—but there were some, inevitably, who could not repress a sharp inner contempt for these newcomers, including even the Europeans, who had crowded into the beloved land not out of pioneering devotion but because of dread of disaster. In the attitude toward the Orientals there was the additional element of fear: they would multiply and overrun the country; they would depress the culture; they would hire themselves out at coolie wages and destroy the high standard of wages achieved by the trade union movement. (This latter fear actually led on occasion to the picketing of camps to prevent the hiring of cheap immigrant labor for work in the citrus groves.)

An otherwise rational Israeli once complained to me, not entirely in sour jest, that "we drove out our good Arabs, and now look at what we have in their place!" While applauding the idea of immigration in the large, many could not help resenting the immigrants themselves —Oriental and European alike—whose presence in the country was the obvious cause of shortages, rationing, and all the other hardships of austerity brought on by the inability of supply to meet the oppressively increasing demand. As for the *sabras*—the tough, cocky young native-born Israelis who took their name from the Palestine cactus and who had never known the sensation of being a displaced Jew—too many of them tended frankly and arrogantly to regard the immigrant as an alien refugee who had not come to Palestine as a heroic volunteer but because he had finally been driven from the lands to which he had cravenly clung.

Nor did the immigrants themselves universally consider the Israelis as beloved brothers, or Israel as a land which was amply fulfilling its promise to them. The true Orientals, notably the Yemenites, found even the wretched reception camps so much more opulent than anything they had ever known that they wanted to stay in them forever. But for many of the others, the chasm between the dream and the reality brought shock, disillusionment and bitterness. And while they ate the hard bread of the homeless stranger, they noted the better conditions and the relative comforts of the Israelis in the thriving cities and the prosperous settlements, and since the complaints by the newcomers to harassed but well-fed officials (also Israelis) seemed to go unheeded, what was more natural than that the immigrant should feel abused and betrayed?

VI / CONCLUSION

29 / THE GLOBAL REDISTRIBUTION OF MAN

In the "boom" that is the modern era of world history, to borrow a term from Walter P. Webb, migration has played a major role, along with trade and conquest and technological advances and other factors. Migration is itself interrelated with all these other forces. Several of them really call for individual treatment, as for example the economics of migration and the theoretical interpretations of human movement. Also, only slight consideration has been given herein to the effect of migration upon migrants' countries of origin through the return of wealth and people and ideas—an aspect hard to analyze but almost as significant as the effect upon receiving countries. Another facet of this modern movement of peoples is the global redistribution of races, which may be its most revolutionary aspect. Professor L. S. Stavrianos of Northwestern University has succinctly summarized this vital phenomenon, and his essay forms an appropriate conclusion for this anthology.

The European discoveries led not only to new global horizons but also to a new global distribution of races. Prior to 1500 there existed, in effect, worldwide racial segregation. The Negroids were concentrated in sub-Saharan Africa and a few Pacific islands, the Mongoloids in Central Asia, Siberia, East Asia, and the Americas, and the Caucasoids in Europe, North Africa, the Middle East, and India. By 1763

Adapted from L. S. Stavrianos, *World History Since 1500* (Englewood Cliffs, New Jersey, 1966), pp. 162–165, 230–235. Copyright © 1966 by Prentice-Hall, Inc. Reprinted by permission of the author and the publisher.

this pattern had been fundamentally altered. In Asia, the Russians were beginning their slow migration across the Urals into Siberia. In Africa the Dutch had established a permanent settlement at the Cape, where the climate was favorable and the natives were too primitive to offer effective resistance. By 1763, 111 years after their landing at Capetown, the Dutch had pushed a considerable distance northward and were beginning to cross the Orange River.

By far the greatest change in racial composition occurred in the Americas. Estimates of the Indian population before 1492 vary tremendously, from 8 million to as high as 100 million. Whatever the figure may have been, there is no disagreement about the catastrophic effect of the European intrusion. Everywhere the Indians were decimated, by varying combinations or physical losses during the process of conquest, disruption of cultural patterns, psychological trauma of subjugation, imposition of forced labor, and introduction of alcohol and of new diseases. Within a century the total indigenous population appears to have declined by 90 to 95 per cent. Most badly hit were the Indians of the Caribbean islands and of the tropical coasts, where they disappeared completely within a generation. More resilient were the natives of the upland tropical regions and of lowland tropical areas such as those of Brazil and Paraguay. Although sustaining very heavy losses, they were able to recover and to constitute the stock from which most of the present-day American Indian population is derived. Only in the twentieth century has this population approached its original numbers in tropical America, while elsewhere it still lags far behind.

The disappearing Indians were replaced by waves of immigrants from Europe and Africa. The resulting settlements were of three varieties. One consisted of the Spanish and Portuguese colonies in which Iberian settlers constituted a permanent resident aristocracy among subjugated Indians in the highlands and imported Negro slaves in the lowlands. Since there were many more men than women among the European immigrants, they commonly took Indian wives or concubines. A mestizo population grew up, which in many parts of the Americas came to outnumber both Europeans and Indians.

A second type of settlement developed in the West Indies, where the Europeans—English and French as well as Spanish—again comprised a resident aristocracy, though with an exclusively Negro imported labor force. At first the planters employed indentured servants from Europe to work their tobacco, indigo, and cotton plantations. But with the shift to sugar in the mid-seventeenth century, much more labor was needed, and slaves were brought over from Africa. In the

British Barbados, for example, there were only a few hundred Negroes in 1640, but by 1685 they numbered 46,000 as against 20,000 whites. The French islands, likewise, had 44,000 Negroes and 18,000 whites by 1700.

The third type of settlement in the Americas was to be found along the Atlantic seaboard. There the native Indians were too sparse or too intractable to serve as an adequate labor supply, and, apart from the southern colonies, the crops did not warrant importing Negro labor. Under these circumstances the English and French settlers cleared the land themselves, lived by their own labors as farmers, fishermen, or traders, and developed communities that were exclusively European in composition.

In conclusion, the mass migrations from Europe and Africa changed the Americas from purely Mongoloid continents to the most racially mixed regions of the globe. Negro immigration continued to the mid-nineteenth century, reaching a total of about fifteen million slaves, while European immigration steadily increased, reaching a high point at the beginning of the twentieth century when nearly one million arrived each year. The net result is that the New World today is peopled by a majority of whites, with substantial minorities of Negroes, Indians, mestizos, and mulattoes, in that order.

The new global racial pattern that resulted from these depopulations and migrations has become so familiar that it is now taken for granted, and its extraordinary significance generally overlooked. What happened in this period to 1763 is that the Europeans staked out claims to vast new regions, and in the following century they peopled those territories—not only the Americas, but also Siberia and Australia. As they expanded territorially so they made possible their own numerical expansion, and they exploited some of the richest resources of the planet. These European Caucasoids came in the 18th to the 20th century to dominate both the areas they populated and much more besides. Taking advantage of the relatively sparse population in the New World, they literally Europeanized North and South America. This could not be done in Asia and Africa, where the indigenous populations were too numerous and highly developed. But in the Americas, and even more in Australia, the Europeans bodily transplanted their civilization in all its aspects—ethnic, economic, and cultural.

The Industrial Revolution was in large degree responsible for this Europeanization. We have seen that increased productivity together with the advances of medical science had led to a sharp increase in

Europe's population in the nineteenth century. This created a population pressure that found an outlet in overseas migration. Railways and steamships were available to transport masses of people across oceans and continents, and persecution of one sort or another further stimulated emigration, the chief example of this being the flight of 1½ million Jews from Russia to the United States in the fifteen years preceding World War I. These various factors combined to produce a mass migration unequaled in human history. With every decade the tide of population movement increased in volume. In the 1820's a total of 145,000 left Europe, in the 1850's about 2,600,000, and between 1900 and 1910 the crest was reached with 9 million emigrants, or almost 1 million per year.

Before 1885 most of the emigrants came from northern and western Europe; after that date the majority were from southern and eastern Europe. By and large, the British emigrants went to the Dominions and to the United States, the Italians to the United States and Latin America, the Spaniards and Portuguese to Latin America, and the Germans to the United States and, in smaller numbers, to Argentina and Brazil. From the perspective of world history, the significance of this extraordinary migration is that it was all directed to the New World and Oceania, with the exception of the large flow to Asiatic Russia and the trickle to South Africa. The result has been the almost complete ethnic Europeanization of North America and Australia. The Indian population in South America managed to survive but was left a minority. In other words, the colonial offshoots of the pre-1763 period now, during the course of the nineteenth century, became new Europes alongside the old.

The Americas and Australia were Europeanized economically as well as ethnically. Before 1763 the European settlements in these continents were confined largely to the coasts. But during the following century the interiors of the continents were traversed. The Industrial Revolution made this overland penetration possible by providing the necessary machines and techniques. The wilderness could not have been tamed without the roads leading inward from the coast, the canals connecting riverways, the railroads and telegraphs spanning continents, the steamers plying rivers and coastal waterways, the agricultural machines capable of cutting the prairie sod, and the repeating rifle that subdued the native peoples. These mechanical aids for the conquest of continental expanses were as essential to Latin Americans and Australians as to American frontiersmen. For example, an Argentinian writing in 1878 observed that "the military power of the

[Indian] barbarians is wholly destroyed, because the Remington has taught them that an army battalion can cross the whole pampa, leaving the land strewn with the bodies of those who dared to oppose it."

The peopling and economic development of the new continents led automatically to the transplanting of European culture as well. It is true that the culture changed in transit. It was adapted as well as adopted. Canada and Australia and the United States today are not identical to Great Britain, nor is Latin America an exact reproduction of the Iberian Peninsula. But the fact remains that the languages are essentially the same, even though Englishmen are intrigued by American slang and Frenchmen by the archaic French-Canadian patois. The religions also are the same, despite the campfire revival meetings and the Mormons. The literatures, the schools, the newspapers, the forms

Principal Sources of European Emigration, 1846–1932

Great Britain and Ireland	18,000,000
Russia	14,250,000 *
Italy	10,100,000
Austria-Hungary	5,200,000
Germany	4,900,000
Spain	4,700,000
Portugal	1,800,000
Sweden	1,200,000
Norway	850,000
Poland	640,000 †
France	520,000
Denmark	390,000
Finland	370,000
Switzerland	330,000
Holland	220,000
Belgium	190,000
TOTAL	63,660,000

Source: A. M. Carr-Saunders, *World Population* (Oxford: Clarendon, 1936), pp. 49, 56; and W. S. and E. S. Woytinsky, *World Population and Production* (New York, Twentieth Century Fund, 1953), pp. 69, 93.

* Consists of 2,250,000 who went overseas, 7,000,000 who migrated to Asiatic Russia by 1914, 3,000,000 who migrated to the Urals, Siberia, and the Far East from 1927 to 1939 and 2,000,000 who migrated to Central Asia from 1927 to 1939. Since 1939, Russian emigration, free and forced, into the trans-Ural areas, has been the greatest single population movement in the world.
† 1920–1932 only.

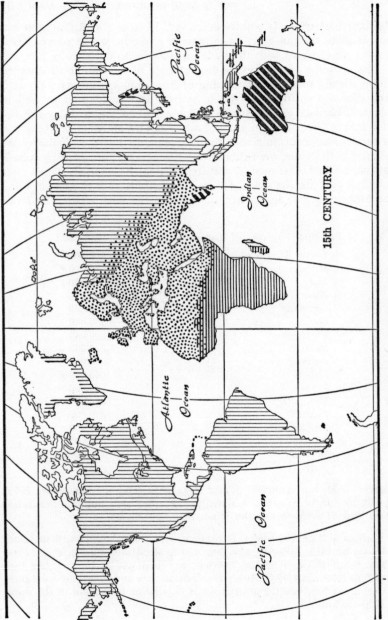

RACIAL DISTRIBUTION IN THE WORLD

15th CENTURY

Pacific Ocean

Indian Ocean

Atlantic Ocean

Pacific Ocean

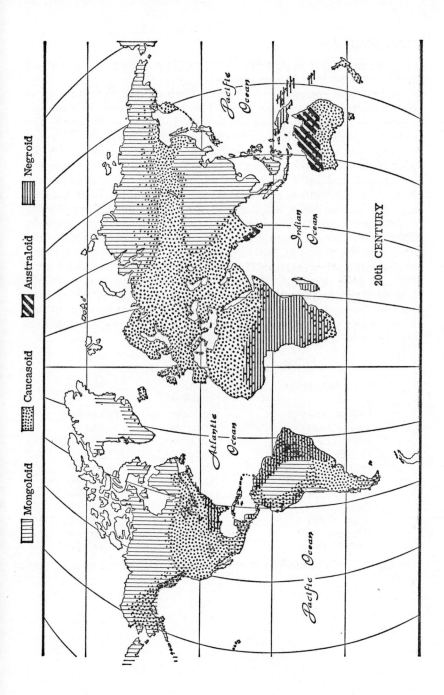

Mongoloid   Caucasoid   Australoid   Negroid

20th CENTURY

Pacific Ocean

Indian Ocean

Atlantic Ocean

Pacific Ocean

of government—all have roots extending back to England and Spain and France and other European countries.

There are, of course, certain cultural strains in the Americas and in Australia that are not European. The Negro element in the New World has retained a certain residue of its African background. The surviving native peoples, especially the Indians in Latin America, are responsible for a hybrid culture. Nor should one forget the impact of the wilderness, leaving its indelible imprint on the European immigrants and on their institutions. All these forces explain why New York, Melbourne, and Toronto are very different from London, and why Buenos Aires, Brazilia, and Mexico City differ from Madrid.

Yet from a global viewpoint the similarities loom larger than the differences. The Arab peoples, in the course of their expansion from their homeland in the Middle East, spread westward across North Africa to the Atlantic Ocean. Today the culture of Morocco is far more different from that of the Arabian Peninsula than the culture of the United States is from that of Britain, or the culture of Brazil from that of Portugal. Yet Morocco is considered, and certainly considers itself, to be a part of the Arab world. In the same sense, the Americas and Australia today are a part of the European world.

Principal Destinations of European Emigration

Destination	Period Covered	Total
United States	1821–1932	34,200,000
Asiatic Russia	1800–1939	12,000,000
Argentina	1856–1932	6,400,000
Canada	1821–1932	5,200,000
Brazil	1821–1932	4,400,000
Australia	1861–1932	2,900,000
British West Indies	1836–1932	1,600,000
Cuba	1901–1932	900,000
South Africa	1881–1932	900,000
Uruguay	1836–1932	700,000
New Zealand	1851–1932	600,000

Source: A. M. Carr-Saunders, *World Population* (Oxford: Clarendon, 1936), p. 49.

FURTHER READING

In addition to the books and articles from which the extracts in this anthology have been chosen—and these works are all worth reading more extensively—there is an almost overwhelming bibliography.

Among the general treatments a good survey is that by Maurice Davie, *World Immigration* (New York, 1936), and a more up-to-date work is Donald Taft and Richard Robbins, *International Migrations: The Immigrant in the Modern World* (New York, 1955). For statistics see the big volume by W. S. Woytinsky and E. S. Woytinsky, *World Population and Production* (New York, 1953). Two stimulating volumes that consider migration within a still larger context of diffusion of culture are Walter P. Webb, *The Great Frontier* (Boston, 1952) and William H. McNeill, *The Rise of the West* (Chicago, 1963).

A good introductory survey is Maldwyn A. Jones, *American Immigration* (Chicago, 1960). On the role of women in the early frontier an interesting special study is Eugenie Andruss Leonard, *The Dear-Bought Heritage* (Philadelphia, 1965). Theodore C. Blegen, *Norwegian Migration to America*, 2 vols. (Northfield, Minn., 1931, 1940), is especially good, universally acclaimed as a model. On the Dutch, see Henry S. Lucas, *Netherlanders in America: Dutch Immigration to the United States and Canada 1789–1950* (Ann Arbor, 1955); for the Irish, Carl Wittke, *The Irish in America* (Baton Rouge, 1956); and for the British, Wilbur S. Shepperson, *British Emigration to North America* (Minneapolis, 1957). A useful more specialized study is that by Rowland T. Berthoff, *British Immigrants in Industrial America 1790–1950* (Cambridge, Mass., 1953). And likewise there are many special writings on the Italians, the Poles, the Germans, the Jews, and others. Very useful for the beginning student is the Localized History Series being edited by Clifford L. Lord, the first three pamphlets being Carl Wittke, *The Germans in America;* Theodore Saloutos, *The Greeks in America;* and Einar Haugen, *The Norwegians in America* (all New York, 1967). These pamphlets include bibliographies.

On Latin American phenomena the *Hispanic American Historical Review* carries occasional articles of relevance, such as James L. Tigner, "The Ryukyuans in Bolivia" (May, 1963) which illustrates both Asian emigration and South American immigration. See also Tigner's book *The Okinawans in Latin America* (Washington, 1955). On Mexican migration see Manuel Gamio, *Mexican Immigration to the United States: a Study of Human Migration and Adjustment* (Chicago, 1930), and on the Puerto Ricans, Oscar Handlin, *The Newcomers* (Cambridge, Mass., 1959).

Works on African migration are accumulating. On the slave trade aspect of the subject see the relevant chapters in U.B. Phillips, *American Negro Slavery* (Gloucester, Mass., 1959); John Hope Franklin, *From Slavery to Freedom: a History of American Negroes,* second ed. (New York, 1965); and Lerone Bennett, *Before the Mayflower: A History of the Negro in America 1619–1962* (Chicago, 1963). Various facets of the purely African aspect of the subject are treated in Polly Hill, *Migrant Cocoa-Farmers of Southern Ghana* (Cambridge, Eng., 1963), and Hilda Kuper, ed., *Urbanization and Migration in West Africa* (Los Angeles, 1965).

For Asian migration an excellent early work is Ta Chen, *Chinese Migrations, with special reference to labor conditions* (Washington, 1923). Good chapters are to be found, also, in Walter F. Willcox, ed., *International Migrations,* 2 vols. (New York, 1931)—Chapter XIX, in Volume II, on "Indian Migration," by G. Findlay Shirras, and Chapter XX, on "International Migration of the Japanese," by Yamato Ichihashi. On the problem of exclusion see Sidney L. Gulick, *The American Japanese Problem: A Study of the Racial Relations of the East and the West* (New York, 1914), and Roy L. Garis, *Immigration Restriction: A Study of the Opposition to and the Regulation of Immigration into the United States* (New York, 1927). Also good is Mary Roberts Coolidge, *Chinese Immigration* (New York, 1909). A significant study of the problems of Japanese migration is Hilary Conroy, *The Japanese Frontier in Hawaii* (Berkeley and Los Angeles, 1953).

Selections in this book deal only occasionally with the complex problems of assimilation, which makes a big subject itself. A good introduction to it is John Higham, *Strangers in the Land: Patterns of American Nativism, 1860–1925* (New Brunswick, 1955). Another approach is to be found in Marion T. Bennett, *American Immigration Policies* (Washington, 1963). A valuable thorough analysis of the process of immigration and assimilation in one Wisconsin county is Merle Curti, *The Making of an American Community* (Stanford, 1959). On this phase of immigration individual memoirs are significant. One of the early ones was Jacob A. Riis, *The Making of an American* (New York, 1902). A recent and beautifully written autobiography of an immigrant scholar is Paul Knaplund, *Moorings Old and New* (Madison, 1963).

Fiction dealing with migration often is not only fascinating, but profoundly revealing. Probably the best of all immigrant novels is Ole Rølvaag, *Giants in the Earth* (New York, 1927), its scene laid in an early Norwegian settlement in South Dakota, but its personalities coming forth as universals. A more all-inclusive story is Wilhelm Moberg's trilogy *The Emigrants* (New

York, 1951), *Unto a Good Land* (New York, 1954), and *The Last Letter Home* (New York, 1962), which portrays a Swedish emigrant group at home in Sweden, in transit, and in process of adjustment in Minnesota. Insight into the meeting of two cultures in East Africa is given by a sensitive and articulate coffee-planter immigrant and author, Isak Dinesen (Karen Blixen) in her *Out of Africa* (New York, 1938).

The economics of migration is another topic that has special significance and its own special studies. One of the best is Brinley Thomas, *Economics of International Migrations* (London, 1958), and his earlier book, *Migration and Economic Growth* (Cambridge, England, 1954). Harry Jerome's *Migration and the Business Cycle* (New York, 1926) was a provocative study that stimulated additional inquiry. Another useful work is Julius Isaac, *Economics of Migration* (London, 1947).

The question of the influence of emigration on the sending country has only recently attracted the attention of scholars. A plea for expanded effort in this field was made at the Stockholm International Congress of Historians in 1960 by Frank Thistlethwaite, whose essay in condensed form is included in Herbert Moller, *Population Movements in Modern European History* (New York, 1964). Among the studies of this kind already made are Theodore Saloutos, *They Remember America: The Story of the Repatriated Greek Americans* (Berkeley and Los Angeles, 1956) and the works of Schrier on Ireland and Gilkey on Italy, mentioned herein. Also the article by F. D. Scott, "Sweden's Constructive Opposition to Emigration," *Journal of Modern History* (Sept. 1965).

Keeping up with the continuous outpouring of books and articles on migration may be done through the *International Migration Review* (Center for Migration Studies, Staten Island, New York 10304) and the *Immigration Research Digest* (Department of Sociology, University of Pennsylvania, Philadelphia 4). Valuable in their own fields are the national group periodicals and publications such as the *German-American Review, The Swedish Pioneer Historical Quarterly, Norwegian American Studies,* and so on.